Economic Myths and
the Mythology of Economics

By the same author:

Introduction to Normative Economics (Oxford University Press, 1981)
Cost–Benefit Analysis: An Informal Approach (Allen & Unwin, 1971)
21 Popular Economic Fallacies (Penguin, 1969)
The Costs of Economic Growth (Penguin, 1967)

Economic Myths and the Mythology of Economics

Ezra J. Mishan

WHEATSHEAF BOOKS

First published in Great Britain in 1986 by
WHEATSHEAF BOOKS LTD
A MEMBER OF THE HARVESTER PRESS GROUP
Publisher: John Spiers
Director of Publications: Edward Elgar
16 Ship Street, Brighton, Sussex

British Library Cataloguing in Publication Data

Mishan, Ezra J.
   Economic myths and the mythology of economics.
   1. Economics
   I. Title
   330   HB171

   ISBN 0-7450-0065-7

1509178

Typeset in Times Roman, 11 point by Eagle Graphics
(Phototypesetting) Limited, Ilkley.
Printed in Great Britain by Billing and Sons Ltd, Worcester

THE HARVESTER PRESS GROUP
The Harvester Group comprises Harvester Press Ltd (chiefly
publishing literature, fiction, philosophy, psychology, and science
and trade books); Harvester Press Microform Publications Ltd
(publishing in microform previously unpublished archives, scarce
printed sources, and indexes to these collections); Wheatsheaf
Books Ltd (chiefly publishing in economics, international politics,
sociology, women's studies and related social sciences); Certain
Records Ltd, and John Spiers Music Ltd (music publishing).

Contents

Prologue

By economic myths I mean beliefs held by economists, or at least by a great majority of them, that cannot be supported by evidence or argument. These myths will not easily be abandoned since they underwrite the self-esteem of the professional economists who believe that their expertise confers substantial benefits on the public and that the results of their research guides the policies of governments in their day-to-day task of steering the economy and their acclaimed long-term goal of raising living standards. In spite of much voguish cynicism, the public tends to share this view and is generally under the illusion that economics is a subject concerned primarily with their material well-being and, in particular, that economic progress ensures that a better life — one richer in opportunity — lies ahead.

Such beliefs encourage people to ignore the evidence of their senses, reflection about which might otherwise disconcert them. By so doing, they allow the greater part of their attention to become absorbed in exciting news items, in current political issues, in the actions and rhetoric of ethnic, feminist and other factions, in local gossip and scandals, in criminal escapades and in foreign coups and revolutions. In the meantime, and while their attention is riveted on such events, our civilization is being persistently and mercilessly undermined by technological innovations and expanding industrial activity. Global environmental destruction continues apace, the number of species of flora and fauna diminish annually, our health is increasingly menaced by new chemical drugs used in foodstuffs, medicines and pesticides, and our cities become ever more vulnerable to breakdown, blackmail and terror. The resulting problems and conflicts of interest continue to produce constricting legislation and so brings us closer to a totalitarian democracy.

Hence the importance of exposing economic myths and of alerting people to the dangers of reposing their hopes for a better life in conventional economic policies which are guided by the conventional economic wisdom. I am not thinking in this connexion about the goals of high employment, price stability and the like, which are the daily bread of our legitimate economic concern. Such concern will certainly continue. But it ought not to blind us to the larger economic issue of secular progress. If we are truly worried about the quality of life, we must first free our minds from traditional economic myths, especially the myth that economic growth of itself entails rising standards of living.

Once free of such economic myths, we have to brace ourselves to the troublesome but far more rewarding task of designing sophisticated policies both for monitoring and controlling technical and scientific innovation, and for devising ambitious programmes for restoring amenity to our towns and cities, for arresting trends towards tasteless vulgarity and for more direct but discriminating measures for improving the quality of our lives.

In this small volume I have included a number of articles and public lectures, written over a period beginning in 1974, selected to offer the reader a sample of the sort of economic myths to which I have addressed myself since the appearance of my *Costs of Economic Growth* in 1967. Each appears as a separate chapter, eight in all, the book itself being divided into three parts. The date and occasion is given below under Acknowledgments. Each essay or public lecture follows the original in every respect apart from the occasional removal or transposition of passages in order to avoid repetition.

June 1985   E.J. Mishan

Acknowledgments

I am grateful to the editors and publishers of the following journals for permission to reproduce the articles that appear in this volume:

Encounter ('The New Inflation', 1974, and 'The Road to Repression', 1976)

Times Literary Supplement (Review of *Inflation: Causes, Consequences, Cures,* London, 1975)

International Review of Law and Economics ('The Effect of Externalities on Individual Choice', 1982)

Political Quarterly ('The Mystique of Economic Expertise', 1984)

National Westminster Bank Review ('GNP: Measurement or Mirage', 1984)

I am equally grateful to the secretaries of the following institutions to reproduce the text of the papers presented to them:

The Fraser Institute, Vancouver ('Religion, Capitalism and Technology', 1983)

The International Conference on Economics and Management, Tokyo 1983 ('The Future Is Worse than It Was', 1983)

PART I

INTRODUCTION

In these first two chapters, I attack the widespread belief among economists, in particular those on the radical right, that inflation is either entirely or primarily a 'monetary' phenomenon, in the sense that the cause of inflation is to be sought in the too-rapid growth of the supply of money. On this view of the matter it must obviously follow that a 'wage-push' explanation is erroneous, being simply an illusion of the untutored lay mind which mistakes the shadow for the substance; in this context, wage-claims being thought to cause a rise in costs when, in fact, such claims are merely the consequent response of workers to the rise in prices that is the result of a 'demand-pull' which arises from the excessive supply of money.

The concomitant belief, held even by economists who have reservations about the monetarist explanation of inflation, is that irrespective of its origin or cause, a restriction in the expansion of the money supply will inevitably bring the inflation to a halt. Technically speaking this is true, given a little time. But it may be politically difficult to adopt a restrictive monetary policy, if only because of the extent of the economic dislocation and political turbulence that would follow in some of the democracies of the West.

The short review article, which is presented as the first chapter, reveals that it was about this time that some monetarists began to incorporate unemployment in a significant way into their explanations of inflation, and to do so by revamping the notion popularised by the 'Phillips curve' of a negative relation between unemployment and the rate of wage increase. According to Friedman's account, this curve has to be transformed into one relating the percentage unemployment to the rate of *increase* in inflation.

So reconciled had economists become to prolonged and rising inflation that the concept of a 'steady state' inflation

3

seemed appropriate enough at the time. This steady-state
inflation entails that the annual percentage increase in the
resulting *real* level of wages be equal to the annual
percentage increase in overall productivity — irrespective
of the magnitude of the constant rate of inflation. And the
unemployment rate that corresponds to this equilibrium or
steady-state inflation is defined by Friedman and others as
'the natural rate of unemployment'. Apparently, and like
the steady-state inflation, it can be of any magnitude.

As it happens, I was unaware of this new adornment to
monetary theory when I wrote my essay (reproduced as
Ch. 2) on the 'New Inflation' two years earlier. But
consideration of such a relationship does not in any way
alter my arguments, and the article appears exactly in the
form it was published in 1974. For this relationship
indicates neither the time necessary for 'the natural rate of
unemployment' to be attained nor the magnitude of this
level of unemployment. Consequently, the concept is bereft
of any instrumental utility. Indeed, as enunciated, the
proposition merely states that the rate of inflation may
continue to rise to some undeterminable level at which it
will increase no further but continue at a constant rate. If
and when it does so, then, during the period of its
constancy, the resultant unemployment is to be defined as
'the natural rate of unemployment'. From this definition we
infer that if the rate of increase of inflation subsides, the
resulting unemployment is to be regarded as being below
this 'natural rate'. The taxonomy, perhaps, is beguiling, but
— apart from letting monetarists off the hook of specific
policy-guidance — the proposition is of no value.

At all events, as readers will note, I was quite explicit
that — contrary to widely accepted economic theory — the
contemporary inflation was predominantly a wage-push
inflation. Moreover, since it was connected in my mind
with a paradigmatic transformation of expectations in the
post-war period, the classical monetary medicine might not
easily work; indeed, I went further and affirmed that only
massive and prolonged unemployment comparable to that
experienced in the inter-war period would check its
impetus. I reflected, finally, that social and political

developments since the Second World War appeared to have brought us to an impasse the nature of which is such that high employment, price stability and traditional free institutions appear no longer to be mutually compatible.

As it turned out, the rate of inflation in the UK and in other countries continued to rise until the end of the decade, reaching rates of over 20 per cent. Nonetheless, the introduction of and persistence in tighter monetary policies by conservative governments did apparently succeed in rolling back the tide of inflation. Within a few years it was pushed back to about 5 per cent. But the price in terms of unemployment was exhorbitant, as I had anticipated.

In view of the rapid changes taking place in productive techniques and the difficulties of retraining displaced workers, it is an open question whether governments today are in fact able to reflate the economy — to reduce unemployment in Britain, for example, to less than one million — even were they prepared to tolerate a significant increase in inflation rates. It is at least as doubtful whether Western economies could reach and maintain high levels of employment again without a recrudescence of two-figure inflation or, alternatively, without effective and far-reaching price and income controls.

1 Demand-pull and Wage-push: Inflation – Causes, Consequences, Cures

What was the cause of the canary's death? Clearly, the cat killed it. But if the canary had been quicker, it would not have been caught. And if the cat had been better fed, it would not have attacked the canary. But, then, if the charwoman had not been so careless as to leave the door open the cat would never have got into the living room. And if the missus had never brought the beastly cat into the home, it could never have happened. One might like to continue in this way for some time rather than conclude that there is no single cause of the canary's death — unless we choose to describe the coincidence of all the pertinent events as itself the cause.

At the conference of which *Inflation* is the record, occasional recognition by Lord Robbins and others of the possibility of getting caught in semantic snarls did not, in the event, prevent some of the participants from making use of language to magnify their differences with others. It is, now, a well-established convention that in all debates bearing on the formation of prices and incomes, the good 'monetarist' must not only disagree with all 'non-monetarists', he must be seen to disagree. And, if a little verbal legerdemain is needed to produce a semblance of disagreement, it will always be forthcoming. Another characteristic of the monetarist style of debate, which was plainly in evidence on this occasion, is a condescending patience in explaining (in the attempt to discredit allegations of trade-union power to raise the level of prices) that a trade union, being a monopolistic organization, is subject also to the same limitations as a monopolistic firm.

7

Star billing at this conference was given to the controversy between Milton Friedman, the veteran monetarist
from Chicago, and Peter Jay, economics editor of *The
Times* — between a highly skilled and articulate professional
on the one hand and, on the other, a prominent and
politically sophisticated financial editor. Although
Professor Friedman enjoyed the ardent (one might even
say aggressive) support of a younger disciple of the Chicago
School, David Laidler of Manchester University, the tepid
support of Sam Brittan of *The Financial Times,* and the
respectful acquiescence of most of the others, the palm in
this debate goes to Mr Jay. Not only were his arguments
forceful and straight to the point, he apparently understood
what his opponents were saying, whereas the impression
left by Professor Friedman and Professor Laidler was that,
carried along by their familiar rhetoric, they did not always
fully appreciate the import of Mr Jay's arguments. The
reader will be better able to assess this opinion after a brief
remark on a recent twist in the development of monetarist
theory.

Although the basic monetarist thesis, of a close
connexion between movements in the money supply and
movements in aggregate income and prices, has not
changed, prior to the development referred to the stability
of product prices was the broad objective of monetary
policy. Conceived as a long-run policy, monetarists
believed that it could be achieved by increasing the supply
of money over time so as to enable average earnings to
grow at a rate equal to the average increase in productivity.
If the increase in money supply were persistently lower
than this stable rate, money earnings would rise at a slower
rate than productivity and the level of prices would fall.
Should the supply of money expand faster than required by
the stable rate, money earnings would rise faster than
productivity, and product prices would rise. Ignoring the
crucial questions of time, of the extent and duration of the
employment-changes involved in making these adjustments
in the level of prices, the role of the monetary authorities
could hardly be simpler — always assuming, of course, that
it is technically feasible under existing institutions for the

authorities to control the supply of money, an assumption that has been challenged recently by the French economist Jacques Melitz. Nonetheless, no economist would seriously dispute the view that any inflation, even a 'wage-push' inflation (however defined), could not continue for a prolonged period without the amount of money in the system continuing to grow.

With the public's attention over the past ten years being increasingly absorbed by inflation, monetary policy has turned to the problem of stabilizing the *rate* of inflation prior to that of stabilizing the *level* of prices. The implications of this shift of focus are easier to understand if, first, we describe the so-called Phillips curve, which made its debut in respectable economic society in 1958. Drawing on annual statistics that covered almost a century of British history, the Phillips curve purposed to reveal a close connexion between the rise in money wages and the level of employment: as the economy approaches full employment, further reductions in unemployment are associated with successively steeper rises in money wages. There is, in addition, some critical level of unemployment, let us say 6 per cent, at which money wages remain stable. It follows that, if overall productivity happens to be increasing at an annual rate of 2 per cent, the existing level of product prices can be maintained simply by choosing that level of unemployment, lower than 6 per cent, for which money wages also rise at 2 per cent per annum.

This simple construct, though happily conceived, was doomed, it seems, to a slow perdition. Curve-fitting is, in any case, a hazardous business in economics, where, as distinct from physics, the universe from which the ultimate parameters are inferred is not likely to remain unchanged for long. Not surprisingly, employers and employees have become increasingly aware over the past decade of the likelihood of higher future prices in wage negotiations, a fact that upsets the original Phillips relationship.

Thus, if prices are generally expected to rise annually at 10 per cent, an annual 3-per-cent increase in real wages would require a 13-per-cent increase in money wages. If overall productivity happens to be increasing at 3 per cent

per annum, well and good. Product prices would then
continue to rise at an annual rate of 10 per cent, and the
rate of inflation would be stable. However, if productivity
were increasing at only 1 per cent, the 13-per-cent rise in
money wages entails a 12-per-cent rise in product prices.
As a result, expectations of future price increases are
revised upwards, from 10 per cent to 12 per cent. A 3-per-
cent increase in real wages now requires a 15-per-cent
increase in money wages. But, if this 15-per-cent wage
increase is granted, the 1-per-cent productivity increase
entails a 14-per-cent rise in product prices, and so on. The
inflation accelerates over time. But what of the level of
unemployment?

With such a mechanism in mind, Professor Friedman
defines a 'natural rate of unemployment' as that which
results in a constant rate of price inflation. This 'steady
rate' inflation, which can be of any magnitude, requires,
therefore, that the annual percentage increase in *real* wages
being granted is exactly equal to the annual increase of
overall productivity.

The immediate policy objective, then, arising from this
view of the economic forces at work, is that of somehow
generating this natural rate of unemployment in order to
stabilize the rate of inflation. Once this is achieved, one
may begin to think about a temporary lowering of the level
of employment below this critical point in the attempt to
reduce the existing magnitude of the steady-rate inflation
— it is hoped, to zero. In effect, Professor Friedman's
analysis can be viewed as a transformation of the Phillips
relationship. The trade-off is no longer that of employment
against rates of wage inflation, but of employment against
increases in rates of price inflation — with zero increase of
the existing inflation rate corresponding to the 'natural rate
of unemployment'.

The movement of the economy towards this critical rate
of unemployment is, then, what is required. And if it is also
believed that this movement can be achieved in no other
way than by curbing the growth of the money supply, then
it necessarily follows that only a restrictive monetary policy
can prevent the inflation gathering momentum.

Before giving the gist of Mr Jay's position, we need to say a word about semantics, if only because the monetarists in this debate averred that the issues separating their views from his were real and important, whereas Mr Jay and, to some extent, Lord Robbins also, believed they were largely semantic. If, in Professor Friedman's explanation of the inflationary process, expectations of future price increases are held exclusively by employers who compete for labour in the market, there need be no hesitation in describing the process as 'demand-pull'.

If, on the other hand, these price expectations are held by employees only, or by employees also — and in his seminal article of 1968 in *The American Economic Review* Professor Friedman in fact says: 'employees will start to reckon on rising prices of the things they buy and to demand higher nominal wages for the future' — it is not so certain. Surely, if in each industry employers concede wage demands in the belief, or hope, that they can always be passed on to the public in higher prices, there is something of wage-push going on. And there can be no doubt that in the current situation the initiative in negotiating wage increases has passed to labour. Indeed, to the extent that Keynes's concept of involuntary unemployment has any validity today, the possibility of there being an excess demand for labour is eliminated even where unemployment is below the natural rate. Whether much of today's unemployment is involuntary or not, however, the insistence on interpreting the current inflation — accompanied as it is by a decline in profits, by an incipient crisis of business confidence, by a collapse of share prices and by growing business complaints of a liquidity shortage — in terms solely of demand-pull, is something of an affirmation of faith.

We are now moving into Jay territory, where the apparent 'pushfulness' of labour is not at all an optical illusion. To Mr Jay, organized labour has in fact been pushing up money wages for some time now in vain attempts to secure, collectively, real earnings beyond the capacity of the economy to support. Other inflations may well have been pure demand-pull inflations; but not this most recent one. Yet Mr Jay goes along with all professional economists in believing that no inflation can continue for long without being fuelled by more and more money. And, what is no less important, he also agrees that if the growth of the money supply does taper off, unemployment will increase and the inflation rate will decline — but as a result of the decline in trade-union militancy, not, as the monetarists would have it, as a result of the decline in the market demand for labour.

Three things can be said in connexion with Mr Jay's analysis of the present inflation in Britain. First, it is at least a coherent and convincing economic explanation of recent events, and one that has a close affinity with the views expressed by quite a number of academic economists on both sides of the Atlantic. It may, of course, turn out to be empirically invalid. But the much-touted 'evidence' of the monetarists cannot sink this kind of model since such evidence is drawn from the past. And evidence from the recent past need not be relevant to the British experience of the past two or three years.

Second, the monetarists themselves do not appear completely to discount the influence of organized labour. According to their own analysis, a reduction in the level of money wages, or a reduction in the existing rate of wage increases, cannot be brought about without some initial, and possibly protracted, reduction in aggregate employment. But if workers were completely passive agents in the market system, no such reduction in aggregate employment would ever occur. In fact the increase in unemployment is a measure of workers' resistance to those downward pressures on existing money wages (or existing money wage increases) that are the result either of direct market forces or of monetary stringency.

This workers' resistance to downward pressures on money wages depends on a number of factors, not excluding trade-union strength. Indeed, in his reply to some questioning by Lord Robbins, Professor Friedman concedes that the existence in the 1920s of strong unions in Britain increased the difficulty there of lowering money wages. Inasmuch as trade-union strength in Britain has grown since then, its influence will be reflected in the larger magnitude of the natural rate of unemployment that the monetarists seek to implement. To that extent, at least, trade-union strength aggravates the political difficulties of tackling inflation.

Whether to claim more than this for organized labour, whether to claim also the power independently to push up wages and prices, is of course the main bone of contention in the debate. But once it is allowed that workers are not passive to market forces, that they do organize effectively to resist wage cuts, or cuts in the rate of wage increases, it is difficult to disallow the possibility that they also organize effectively to push up wages.

Incidentally, the attempts by monetarists to refute allegations of trade-union power to raise wages by labouring the similarities between a monopoly firm and a trade union cannot be taken seriously. The issue is not whether a single union can do anything more than increase its share of the wage-bill; the issue is whether, *in the attempt,* within a short span of time, of each of many unions to increase its real wage or to improve its wage differential in the wage structure, a general rise in the level of prices can be generated. The analogy between trade unions and private corporations would hold only in a world in which the private corporations persistently claimed a rise in the prices of their products by reference to the profit earnings of other firms, threatening lock-outs if their demands were rejected. If they competed with one another to push up their profits by raising their prices, the price level could indeed move upwards; that is, by acting like trade unions, they too could engineer an inflation — assuming, of course, in both cases, adequate accommodation by the monetary authority.

Third, although the policy options that emerge from one particular analysis of a situation can, in general, differ from those that emerge from another analysis, the conflict of views over the role of organized labour in the current inflation did not, as it happens, prevent the emergence of a common alternative to continuing inflation: an increase of unemployment through monetary restriction. Mr Jay, however, would be disposed to supplement this policy by wage and price controls, an option that is anathema to the monetarists. Yet the choice between policies is not a purely theoretical matter; it tends to be doctrinal. It ought to be pragmatic.

At all events, none of the participants in the debate dissociated himself from the belief that once *enough* unemployment is created, the current inflation will abate its force. In that important respect, then, there was *de facto* agreement, notwithstanding the sectarian propensities of the monetarists or their ritual insistence that the *cause* of inflation (the emphasis is Laidler's) is simply monetary expansion; or to give Professor Friedman's more revealing version: 'the fundamental cause' of inflation is 'the attempt to use a monetary weapon to fix something which it cannot fix'; namely, virtually full employment with price stability.

When pressed, later, on this question of causation by Lord Robbins, Professor Friedman was more cautious. He agreed that the word 'cause' was unsatisfactory. He himself, he declared, preferred to speak of changes in the money supply as 'a proximate cause', and he went on to mention 'the deeper causes' that 'must be found in what are the explanations for the rise in the money supply'. But this sort of explanation is just what Mr Brittan was concerned with when he talked of the need to incorporate 'political realism' into the economic models. What is more, it is just the sort of explanation that Mr Jay is offering for the continued growth in the money supply. He takes as his text a caveat written into a passage of the monetarists' 'Dear Prime Minister' pamphlet of 1974. In reflecting the notion of trade-union power as a cause of inflation, they wrote:

If the increase of union wages induces the authorities to expand the money supply either to finance public expenditure designed to reduce any concomitant unemployment or to finance the deficits of nationalised industries, then such action will indeed be inflationary. It is simply not possible for the trade unions to be so powerful as to cause prices to rise generally unless there is concomitant increase in the money supply. No one has ever produced any evidence to the contrary.

Now this penultimate sentence clearly implies that, if there is 'a concomitant increase in the money supply', then it is possible 'for the trade unions to be so powerful as to cause prices to rise generally'. And Mr Jay is saying quite plainly that there has been, and still is, this 'concomitant increase in the money supply' just because British governments are politically committed to maintain high levels of employment. A comparison of this conclusion with Professor Friedman's version of the 'fundamental cause' of the inflation quoted above — in effect, the attempts of governments, through their monetary policies, to maintain a level of employment higher than is consistent with price stability — surely vindicates my earlier remark that the monetarists did not always fully appreciate the import of Mr Jay's arguments.

A democratic government sensitive to electoral opinion and pledged to maintain full employment has little room for manoeuvre in the current situation. It is aware — as which of us is not? — that the continuing attempts to secure real gains, which in the aggregate exceed the growth of real national output, can only fan the flames of inflation. Yet fearful of the political consequences of the unemployment that would ensue if it squeezed the money supply, or if it reduced its excess expenditure, the government chooses, albeit uneasily, to go along with inflation. This 'deeper' explanation is plausible enough. It leaves out nothing but an answer to the question: why did it not happen before 1970?

We may well conclude that in a democratic society, at least an affluent one with a highly developed communications system, price stability and full employment cannot easily be reconciled with two of its current institutions, free collective bargaining and (if I may add it myself) the welfare state. And no credit accrues to the monetarists' case when, apprehending the possibility of a political dilemma, Professor Friedman exorcizes it by describing it as a source of *explosion* rather than as a source of *inflation*. It makes for clearer thinking, surely, to perceive the cause of the inflation as residing in this dilemma; in the apparent irreconcilability of current aspirations with current institutions.

In the light of this conclusion, it looks as if something has to go. But if, in the event, price stability is sacrificed, in particular if something like the present rate of inflation goes on for a few more years then — at least in the absence of widespread indexing — liberal democracy may have to go with it. This pessimistic assessment of the situation is not, incidentally, confined to Mr Jay.

What of the monetarists' solution, unemployment? The natural rate of unemployment required merely to stabilize the inflation could be excessive in the light of current aspirations. The monetarists could not put a finger on it. It might not be less than one million. It could be more, especially if the official target was that of reducing the inflation rate to some tolerable figure, say, something below 5 per cent.

In the circumstances, the advice blandly given to seemingly obtuse governments by some monetarists, that the growth of the money supply be reduced to damp down the inflation, looks about as promising a political idea as that of the young mouse in the fable who created quite a stir by proposing a bell be tied around the cat's neck.

Indeed, official vacillation in applying monetary restriction can be rationalized even when the policy proposed follows Professor Friedman's prudent prescription of a slow but persistent pressure on the growth of the money supply. For we have accumulated much scepticism over the years about the economists' skill in the art of 'fine tuning'. There is some apprehension that, even if initially successful, the recession we carefully engineered might slip beyond our control into a prolonged depression.

The temptation is to procrastinate. There is always the possibility that some providential happening might rescue us from the existing predicament. A decline in world food and commodity prices that would turn the terms of trade in Britain's favour would be such an event. But we should not be wise to count on it. In the meantime, what to do?

If one is pessimistic about the extent of the unemployment needed to overcome the current inflation, or about the ability of our democratic institutions to withstand two-digit inflation for much longer, ideas about introducing a longish period of wage and price controls are sure to have some political appeal. Professor Friedman agreed that such controls worked in the Argentine because, among other factors, people were convinced that the government was in earnest. Such controls work imperfectly however, and it is not hard for an economist to pour scorn on them and to make dark allusion to those sinister 'distortions' about whose magnitude and potential welfare loss he knows very little. But, as Professor Friedman himself says, we are not living in a 'first best' world, and if the stark alternatives — inflation or unemployment — are as politically dangerous as Mr Jay and others think, the proposal of a longish spell of wage and price controls, as one device among others that might contain both inflation and unemployment, deserves closer consideration than it currently receives from academic economists.

It would be unfair to end this review of a fascinating report without mention of Professor Friedman's lucid exposition of the advantages of voluntary and official indexing as a means of redressing the inequities of inflation, without a tribute to the brief historical introduction by Professor Coats that is wise and witty and nicely sceptical, and without also acknowledging the high qualities of Lord Robbins as chairman of the conference. His opening remarks put the debate in proper perspective and, while continually active in shunting people's thoughts onto the right tracks and making astute observations himself, he managed to keep the peace among an unusually lively group.

2   The New Inflation:
Its Theory and Practice

The unending debate on the causes of inflation ranges from explanations of pure 'demand-pull' (or excess spending) to those depending exclusively on the notion of 'cost-push' (excessive pay claims). There is always a temptation to make judicious statements about the need for a realistic view of the phenomenon to contain elements of both theories. Yet it is a fact that among professional economists, certainly among academic economists, the debates on inflation tend to cluster about the demand-pull end of the spectrum.

This is understandable for two related reasons. All known inflations, both in modern and ancient history, have apparently been of the demand-pull variety, and (as Professor Milton Friedman reminds us from time to time) such inflations are easiest to explain in terms of unusual expansions of the supply of money. The other reason is that only a demand-pull explanation fits comfortably into traditional economic theories of price and income determination. All such theories favour classical liberal remedies that preclude 'direct' government intervention and tend to favour monetary and fiscal policies which act 'indirectly' on the economy at large.

What of the differences of opinion and doctrine among professional economists themselves? They have turned on the relative importance of the effect on aggregate money income of, on the one hand, changes in overall expenditure, and of changes in the overall supply of money on the other. These differences in theory are translatable into differences in policy that emphasise, respectively, fiscal controls and monetary controls. Since British governments over the last few years have been increasing the supply of money at an annual rate of anything up to 30 per cent and, in the last two years in particular, have been running sizable budgetary deficits, the inflationary outcome is consistent with both versions of the demand-pull theory. The statistical evidence is insufficient to exclude either.

Inasmuch as the attention of the general public is attracted more to the vivid incidents of industrial strife than to monthly variations in the quantity of money, or to estimates of budgetary deficits, the ordinary citizen is predisposed to a 'wage-push' explanation of today's rising prices — even though he máy concede, on occasion, that workers are only attempting to resist a decline in their living standards following, say, a rise in the price of food imports. And however the Treasury or the Bank of England view of the matter is interpreted, the recent policies of British governments suggest a strong attachment to the same cost-push hypothesis. For while huge budget deficits[1] have been incurred and the economy flooded with money, governments have sought to control the price level by direct intervention in what would otherwise be free collective bargaining — by sporadic 'freezes', by income policies, by direct negotiations with trade unions, and (in desperation) sometimes by public appeals.

After so signal a failure to arrest the upward spiral of prices, one might reasonably hope that, sooner or later, governments would become more amenable to the arguments advanced by professional economists and others to the extent of trying to implement the policies they continue to propagate. Since the prospect is far from impossible, it behoves us to press the question that most economists today would regard as impertinent. Would stricter monetary and fiscal controls indeed suffice, in existing circumstances, to curb inflation and restore price stability?

A few years ago, I would have dissociated myself from any explanation of inflation couched primarily in terms of union militancy, and from any policy involving direct intervention in the process of collective bargaining.

I would have gone along with the orthodox economic view: even where an inflation is not caused by excess expenditures, public or private, it can be checked by appropriate monetary and/or fiscal measures. I hasten to add, however, that I still believe that such measures would have been effective before the Second World War and would probably have worked well enough until around the mid-1960s. They would not, I think, be successful today. But if the last government happened to be right in regarding the demands of organised labour as the major obstacle to any attempt to damp down the inflationary pressure, it is also true that the policies pursued by successive governments have done much to intensify a militancy among the working class that is, in the last resort, the product of more general economic forces.

Thus the role of governments (particularly in Britain), both in aggravating post-war inflations and in making them increasingly resistant to ordinary monetary and fiscal controls, is worthy of detailed commentary. But such detailed commentary is better appreciated after a description of the developments associated with the new inflation, developments that spring from a single phenomenon: sustained economic growth. Although these growth-inspired developments have been at work since the turn of the century or earlier, it is only in the last few years that they have combined to provide organised labour with a will and power effective enough to thwart the operation of traditional economic nostrums.

THE INFLATION PROCESS

Impatient as I am to broach my main thesis, there are certain economic facts of life which bear on the experience of a prolonged period of rising prices and which, though not essential to this main thesis, certainly compound the difficulties of controlling the new inflation. Let me first touch upon three of such facts lest I be accused of unduly simplifying the issue.

(1) Productivity Differences Between Industries.
In the nature of things, technological advances occur more rapidly in some industries than in others, with the result

that, irrespective of the individual efforts of the workers concerned, output per man-hour advances faster in the former. Over a thirty-year period, for instance, we should expect to discover a significant rise in the productivity of steel workers but no significant rise in that of hairdressers. Granted this fact of life, how does one cope? One policy, at once equitable and non-inflationary would be that of maintaining money wages roughly unchanged in all occupations while allowing increases in productivity, wherever they happen to occur, to be translated into *commensurate price reductions*. In this way, the benefits of each and every technical or managerial innovation are *spread* throughout society as soon as they occur.

Alas, historical developments have brought about institutions that foster quite contrary results. As we now know, if productivity in the machine-tool industry rises by, say, 8 per cent on the average each year, workers there will assert a right, in effect, to appropriate the *whole* of the improvement by demanding pay increases of at least 8 per cent per annum. Of course, if in every sector of the economy productivity were also advancing at about 8 per cent per annum, such claims could be met without causing problems. Instead of prices everywhere falling by about 8 per cent with money incomes unchanged (an outcome that would result from following the more equitable policy mentioned above), all workers' incomes would now rise by 8 per cent with prices remaining constant.

But, as indicated, this uniform advance in productivity does not take place. Indeed, there are some economic activities that fail to register any productivity gains. One thinks, in this connexion, of some of the service industries — in the advanced industrial countries, they tend to grow as a proportion of national output — in which the measurable productivity of the bulk of the employees (consisting of office workers, salesmen, receptionists, teachers, journalists, actors and others) does not change from one year to the next. Yet they, too, in the modern world, will expect pay increases over time comparable with those gained by employees in the technically advancing sectors of the economy.

The inflationary potential of this situation is easily illustrated. Imagine that the aggregate incomes of the employees in the service sectors, which show no productivity gains, make up about half the total income of the economy, and the remaining employees in the industrialised sectors account for the other half. If the productivity of the latter sectors is 8 per cent, then for the economy as a whole it is 4 per cent. But if the service workers, following the example of the industrialised workers, claim and receive an 8 per cent increment in their money incomes, then *all* money incomes are raised by 8 per cent while overall productivity — or the real output of the economy — has increased by only 4 per cent. Since the rise in money incomes now exceeds the rise in real output by 4 per cent, prices will rise by about 4 per cent.[2]

If workers become aware of this rise in prices — and, today, you can safely assume as much — their next pay claim will take into account the 4 per cent increase in the cost of living. And so, in the absence of countervailing policies (and with productivity gains continuing to concentrate in the industrial sectors) the process gathers momentum as expectations of future price increases now enter into pay claims.

(2) The Tax Structure.
The growth of average money-incomes over time shifts income-earners into higher tax brackets and yields revenues to the government that form a rising proportion of national income. This growth in the proportion of government revenues arises (even if prices remain constant over time) simply as a result of the secular growth in per capita 'real' income, and it offers strong political temptations to expand the range of state activities.

The faster the rate of inflation, the larger is the proportion of national income that accrues to governments, and — provided, always, that public alarm at the pace of inflation is not widespread — the greater the wherewithal at their disposal, a result which enables them occasionally to pose as the custodians of the public interest; for the 'windfall' tax revenues, arising from their *failure* to restrain prices and money incomes, can be passed off as evidence of prudent budgeting. It is then possible to court political popularity on the Right and on the Left by using the windfall revenues both to reduce tax rates and to increase public expenditure.

This phenomenon is well known to economists, and there have been a number of studies designed to estimate the real increase in government revenues for every 1 per cent rise in aggregate money income.[3] What is emerging for the first time, however, is the responsiveness of workers not to their *gross* incomes but — having been pushed by prolonged inflation into the income-tax range — to their *disposable* incomes or 'take-home pay'. As a corollary, their pay claims have become inflated.[4] For if average weekly earnings are between £35 and £40, workers facing a 10 per cent inflation will require increases in their gross income of between 12 and 14 per cent (depending on family size, etc.) in order simply to maintain their real spending.

(3) International Trade.

The greater a country's dependence upon international trade, the more prone it is to import an inflation from abroad (at least if its exchange-rate is held constant). If, for example, the British economy were infected by foreign inflations, its exports to the inflationary countries would rise, its imports from them would fall, and pressures would build up to appreciate the value of the pound. This could happen, but it has not been happening. Britain's rate of inflation is, in fact, somewhat above the average for the industrialised countries.

Nonetheless, the relative prices of a few important international goods (foodstuffs, oil and some metals) have risen sharply over the year, but not so much from the result of inflation as of incipient world shortages that may or may not continue. In less crisis-prone times, this event would be manageable. World prices are continually changing. Provided exchange rates are flexible enough, the balance of payments looks after itself, and the higher costs of some items would be borne philosophically. But these are not ordinary times. The rise in food prices over the years has been steep enough to make a noticeable dent in living standards of a lot of people, and this at a time when we have become conditioned to expect a continuing improvement of our living standards from year to year.

As result of political and economic events beyond our control, real income in Britain will not be greater this year than last year, and could be somewhat smaller. Indeed, in view of the possibility of unforeseeable political developments in countries from which we buy and sell, in view also of possible crop failures, ecological disasters, technological disappointments and perhaps also (because of increasing world population) of a secular rise in the relative price of foodstuffs, it would be foolish to encourage a belief that the present interruption to rising prosperity can only be temporary and that we can reasonably anticipate a quick resumption of its continuance. Looking beyond the present crisis, then, persistent refusal in Britain (and in other countries) to accept economic limitations and to adjust our expectations to more modest rates of growth in the future, could only plunge us deeper into inflation.

THE GROWTH OF EXPECTATIONS

Let me now turn to the main thesis concerning the link between economic growth and the new inflation.

Although the imperial conception of sustained economic growth harks back to Adam Smith or earlier, it was only during the nineteenth century that the idea of 'perpetual progress' was pervasive enough to become a tacit presumption about the workings of Providence. From the mid nineteenth century until very few years ago, the predominant opinion among social philosophers, businessmen, economists and reformers, whether of the Right or Left, was that material conditions were sure to continue to improve over time. But until about the middle of this century, the mass of working people did not share this optimistic view of things. Despite the enthusiasm of the 'intelligentsia' about the unlimited potential of science and technology, the ordinary working man was not given to thinking of the economic system as something powered by a growth engine that, when properly tended, must continuously and perceptibly increase the material wealth of society (to which increase of wealth, incidentally, the working class had a rightful claim). Indeed, as recently as the inter-war period, the overriding aim of the average worker was to find and to hold onto a job. And if the capitalist system came under fire from the Left, it was largely because that system appeared to be constitutionally unable to provide all willing workers with remunerative employment. According to the standard socialist criticism, the system was inherently wasteful as well as unjust. The Western world was littered with abandoned farms, factories and mines, and everywhere there were armies of idle, bitter and demoralised men.

In sharp contrast to the economic situation of the 1930s, the post-war era has been one of strong political, indeed electoral, emphasis on high employment and material growth in all the industrialised nations.

Five years of active post-war reconstruction merged into a prolonged period of prosperity. From it was born the notion of economic growth as the singular and self-evident goal of national policy and, by gradual extension, as the natural metric of national achievement and the sovereign remedy for all social disorders. Its active encouragement became the central concern of successive governments in all countries. The concern soon became an obsession, one that expressed itself in widely publicised schemes for improving economic performance, in plans to achieve growth targets and in new institutions designed to promote productivity. It was reflected in recurrent forecasts and comparisons of real per capita GNP. Not surprisingly, such developments have fostered expectations of increasing plenty that are exaggerated and almost certainly unrealisable.

When, following the 'pay pause' of 1961, the National Economic Development Council was launched amid much fanfare in 1962, it soon came up with a statement, which received the widest publicity, about Britain's ability to maintain an average growth rate of 4 per cent. I recall asking the late Professor Eli Devons what good he thought such a declaration could do. His prompt reply was to the effect that it would impress on the labour unions an argument for demanding an average annual pay increase of at least 4%, and thus would make a sensible contribution to the existing inflationary pressure. And, indeed, union sensitivity was such that a mention in the first 'Neddy' report of the need for rapid expansion of the building industry was followed by the largest wage claim in its history. Since then:

a variety of policies, all under the umbrella term 'prices and income policies', have been proposed in the UK to control inflation. They have ranged from a statutory control of wages and prices, a national body for settling wage disputes, a voluntary prices and incomes policy, a tax on wage demands above a stated percentage, a national job evaluation scheme, and the enunciation of a 'norm' for wage and price increases.[5]

During the years 1965 to 1970 no less than six White Papers appeared, each offering different criteria by which to assess prices and pay claims.

Thus, during the same decade over which a succession of ineffectual anti-inflationary pie-sharing schemes were being hatched by governments, the public was subjected to an intermittent hot-and-cold treatment, made restless with visions of burgeoning GNPs, and disquieted by a torrent of invidious statistics bearing on differentials as between occupations, on changes in the cost of living, and on per capita 'real' earnings within and between countries.

The inevitable consequences of these growth-inspired developments has been to engender a quite unprecedented hypersensitivity among occupational groups throughout the country on the issue of their share of the national pie — or, more exactly, of the increase in their members' earnings as compared with the increase in the earnings of members in other occupations. One instance of this growing touchiness of the unions to the cost of living (and to relative position) occurred with the setting up of the Prices and Incomes Board of 1968. The event was soon followed by a round of exorbitant wage claims. Each union was anxious to submit and settle its claim before 'the doors closed' and, also, to allow itself plenty of margin both for bargaining with the

Board and for anticipated increases in the cost of living.

The Heath government's Income and Prices Policy, and its operative phases, One, Two and Three, undoubtedly acted to aggravate further the scramble among the unions, among the shop stewards and workers, to squeeze the most out of employers and the government. The fact that real wages today are calculated to be about twice as high as those prevailing in the 1930s has no deterrent effect whatever. What matters are the comparisons as of now. And everybody in Britain knows by now that real earnings in most of Western Europe are higher than those here, and that in America they are about twice as high as they are in this country. British officials have repeatedly referred to such statistics, and the newspapers never cease to remind the citizen of them. He also reads and hears about large speculative gains, of record sums being spent on foreign travel and on popular entertainment, decent and indecent. Above all, each segment of organised labour is acutely aware that the widget-makers union managed to negotiate a 17 per cent increase six months ago, that the bookbinders brotherhood got an extra £4.50 some eight months ago, and so on.

Under the impact of post-war events that can trace their origin to the Establishment's absorbing concern with economic growth, the workers of Britain (and of other Western countries also) are fast being transformed into a corps of pay-vigilantes.

WHY TRADITIONAL ECONOMIC REMEDIES MAY NOW BE INEFFECTIVE

Granted that the quickening response of the public to years of unabating growthmania has brought us to this frantic state in which we can scarcely digest our allotted slice of the pie for glowering at the slices being eaten by others, why cannot economists advise governments on practical measures for bringing pressure to bear on the growing avalanche of wage claims? Why, in other words, may it no longer be possible to apply fiscal and monetary measures so as eventually to stabilise prices or, at least, reduce significantly the rate of inflation experienced over the last two or three years?

A small part of the answer is to be found in the larger units of production that are promoted by those narrowly conceived considerations of efficiency which come to the fore in optimistic periods of rapid economic expansion. Variety and small scale are part of the ecological prescription for systems-stability. They should perhaps be part also of the economist's prescription. A city or region that comes to depend wholly on one or a few sources of supply for some vital service such as electricity, water, gas, sewage disposal or public transport, is clearly more vulnerable than one that can call on a larger number of smaller sources. This is particularly so in an age in which news media give prominence to the occasional escapades of fanatic urban-guerrilla groups skilled in blackmail and havoc. We are beginning to realise that the economies-of-scale from larger plant size may be dearly paid for in terms of increased social hazard.

A larger part of the answer may be found in the growing power of organized labour over the last thirty years, and its awareness of that power. The ease with which the trade unions (or, for that matter, any determined group of workmen) are able to exert pressure on employers and on the public has, of course, been facilitated by the larger size of industrial plant, itself a product of technical advance, and also by nationalising such 'key' industries as coal, steel, electricity generation and rail transport. But even without any growth in the size of industrial plant or in the extent of nationalisation, it would not be reasonable to suppose that with the rapid expansion of communications, action by workers would continue to be confined to particular firms or localities.

A strike against a single firm is not so effective (unless it happens to be in a strong monopoly position) as a strike against all employers in the industry, and this is so for two reasons. First, the single firm will choose to close down rather than so to increase its wage costs as to be unable to compete in the market for its products — whereas if all firms in the industry grant a sizable wage-increase, the additional cost can be passed on to the public in the form of higher prices without much loss in sales volume. Second, any disruption of the flow of products or services from the industry as a whole, whether by strike action, 'working to rule', or other method, will be suffered by the general public who, it is assumed, will always favour a speedy settlement through existing arbitration machinery or, in the last resort (and the last resort is never far off today), through government intervention.

In a liberal democratic society, no political party wants to be associated by the electorate with continued industrial unrest or prolonged inconvenience (especially if an election is in the offing). And since it also does not wish its term of office to be associated with severe and protracted unemployment, the government of the day is tempted to seek concessional formulas rather than lay off workers in the face of exhorbitant demands.

Thus, even without the broad sympathy and tacit support of the sizable proportion of the parliamentary Labour Party — which some London political commentators have made much of — the labour unions are in a strong position *vis-à-vis* any elected government, and particularly so in those sectors of the economy where a withdrawal of labour at once reduces essential services. It is hardly surprising, then, that in the atmosphere of economic opportunism created by growth-men over the last thirty years, workers are not above using their organised power pretty ruthlessly, or, as they might put it, 'realistically'.

The above interpretation of recent events is not likely to ruffle anyone unduly. But its significance has not been fully appreciated, least of all by economists whose explanations of the resulting inflation runs primarily in terms of inept monetary and fiscal policies.

I am suggesting that the monetary inflation cannot properly be understood without recognising its connexion with the universal inflation of expectations that has characterised the history of the post-war world. Seen in that light it appears as a product, possibly an inevitable product, of the evolution of the capitalist ethic.

The liberal economist with his faith in material progress as the prime solvent of all social problems is, of course, aware that the restless spirit of discontent fostered by nineteenth-century capitalism has today diffused itself throughout the world. But he still tends to see this phenomenon as a positive source of social good inasmuch as the resulting struggle for material advancement is (he believes) channelled into sustained effort, and into innovation and ingenuity, which, over time, redound to the public benefit in the form of rising levels of prosperity.

And so it would if this spirit of discontent and acquisition raged only in the breasts of the bourgeoisie, or — in the twentieth century — in the breasts of managers, technocrats and professionals. But once this spirit takes possession of the masses, a socially beneficent outcome is no longer assured. For their own attempts at material self-betterment need not follow the path of economic virtue depicted by the liberal economist. Indeed, it does not do so. Instead, these attempts take the form of large-scale group action designed, not to contribute more to the size of the national pie, but simply to appropriate a larger share of it. Each union-organised group will of course continue to talk about 'productivity', about 'fairness' about 'the national interest', about 'proper differentials' and 'the structure of the industry', these terms being a part of the political language of negotiation. But each realises that the concessions it can wring from society depend ultimately on the extent of the potential disruption it can inflict on the community.

In these circumstances the standard economic medicine may no longer work — and not only because, with the introduction of tolerable unemployment benefits, wages are resistant to any downward pressure. Money wages were pretty rigid even before the Second World War, as Keynes was then at pains to emphasise. In the present inter-union race to keep ahead of the cost of living, and to keep ahead of each other, wage levels cannot but escalate. A pattern of union militancy is emerging which threatens to be independent of demand conditions. Thus fiscal policy alone may be of no avail. Nor yet monetary policy, which though its allocative effects differ (working, as it does, directly through restrictions in bank lending and also indirectly through higher interest rates and capital losses), likewise acts initially through a reduction of aggregate spending.

The orthodox argument is that a refusal by the authorities to expand the quantity of money any further, or their determination to reduce the quantity of money, will eventually make it impossible for employers to grant wage increases even if they are otherwise willing to do so. But if, following such a contingency, workers (though aware of the financial inability of the industry to meet their wage claims) remain adamant in 'working to rule', or in refusing to return to work, what then? With the central bank under the control of the government of the day, their persistence in strike action has now to be interpreted as a form of direct pressure on the government to relax its monetary decisions. And in Britain, where more than a half of the country's total economic activity is directly under the control of the government, such pressure can be pretty effective.

In the absence of wide-ranging controls on capital and labour (which are thought to be politically unacceptable except in dire emergencies) one does not have to be a pessimist to suspect that only *prolonged and widespread unemployment,* comparable with that experienced in the 1930s, would today suffice to break the psychological momentum acquired by the inflationary process over the last two decades.

In sum, then, successive governments, in their monomaniacal pursuit of economic growth, have sown the seeds of discontent among their peoples and are now reaping a bitter harvest. The unabating struggle for 'more' between the unions (white collar no less than blue collar) has become more defiant over the last several years. In American cities there have been strikes of doctors and of policemen; in British cities, strikes of nurses, firemen, ambulance men and school teachers.

The counter-pressure that the authorities can exert is limited. Legislation to withdraw unemployment benefits from workmen officially on strike would be politically unpopular, and it might well unite the unions against any government contemplating it. Attempts by government

spokesmen, editorial writers and columnists to arouse the
indignation of the public against alleged irresponsibility are
generally ineffectual. For the defiant workmen do not see
themselves primarily as members of a larger political
community held together by a common history and by a
network of rights, customs and obligations. The very idea
of nationhood is made obsolescent by technological progress, by instant international communications, by mass
mobility and by supra-national aspirations arising from a
growing consciousness of economic and ecological inter-
dependence. The members of the union, on such occasions,
see themselves rather as a fraternity asserting their claims
against those of others. If the public, following the lead of
the government and the press, evinces disapproval of their
action, they simply close ranks and derive moral sustenance
from their comradeship and their common cause.

PLAYING DICE WITH THE ECONOMY

Ten years ago the order of inflation in Britain was between
3 and 5 per cent. Today it has begun to pass the 10-per-cent
figure and approaches a take-off into strato-inflation.

   On taking office, the Heath government, though it
shared the general alarm at the pace of inflation, put the
pursuit of faster economic growth before the goal of price
stability. Despite the portents, it decided to take a gamble
and — with what looks in retrospect like unwarrantable
optimism — hoped to avert a rise in the rate of inflation by a
rise in the rate of economic growth. It was as if the
government, having unwittingly succumbed to its own
growth propaganda, had begun to think of Britain, not in
terms of a complex social order, but in terms of a gigantic
business corporation. At the helm of Britain Incorporated,
Mr Heath was evidently convinced that a gamble with the
currency was justified if there were fair prospects of some
larger dividend being earned by the Old Firm. Against all
the evidence of past experience, he later hoped that his
incomes policy, supplemented by frequent invocations of
'the national interest', would be effective in holding back

the continued inflationary pressure until there would be goodies enough to satisfy everybody. World events have, of course, played some part in precipitating the current malaise. But considering the mood of organised labour, and the government's monetary and fiscal policies of the last two years, only the most unlikely constellation of propitious events could have averted the ensuing crisis.

In particular, the fond vision of an 'export-led growth' (in outline similar to that which was experienced by Germany during the 1950s and early 1960s) tempted the Heath government into the present wilderness. One can, incidentally, just as well envisage an 'import-led growth' taking place in Germany or elsewhere, or, for that matter a 'trade-balanced growth'. Nevertheless, we can ignore the 'export-led' aspect of the economic growth objective — which, if realised, has the incidental effect of increasing our overseas assets by reducing the domestic supply of goods, so making it more inflationary than its counterpart, 'import-led growth'. For the anti-inflationary contribution to be had from rapid economic growth itself arises essentially from the productivity increases that enable workers to receive higher wages without the prices of goods having to rise or to rise very much.

The dash for economic growth was not a good gamble. Although the Establishment is loath to admit it, the ability to determine the rate of the economy's growth during the next year or two — as distinct from the ability to promote policies that are believed to encourage economic growth — is beyond the power of governments. It would be so even if the economy were not subject to international forces. For a number of reasons any one can adduce, but no one can be quite sure of, the UK has since the war settled down to an average growth rate approaching 3 per cent, as measured by the conventional indices. The government can, of course, announce its intentions of trying for a 4 or 5 per cent growth rate, and make a lot of busy noise in the process. But no one is at all surprised if it turns out to be only 1 or 2 per cent after all. There are always those ubiquitous world forces to play with in any post-mortem, to say nothing of 'sluggish management' or 'structural perversities'.

Now, as events would have it, something that (on recent information) looked like a 5 per cent growth rate was in fact achieved in the year ending about mid-1973. But the greater part of this apparent growth can be attributed, not to any significant productivity gains (which is what growthmen are really after) but to the re-employment of about half-a-million British workers. Although this is undoubtedly a good thing, it is not exactly what is wanted in the way of margin for meeting wage claims. Indeed, the increase in employment for itself added something to the import bill, and thus worsened Britain's balance of payments, which was already suffering from the sharp increase in world prices of foodstuffs and minerals.

The government was of course hoping for a slide in the world prices of raw materials which, had it occurred, would not only have relieved the balance of payments deficit but would also have reduced the cost of living. But it was not to be.

The forces that combine to produce the new inflation are, as I have argued, such as to render it intractable to the usual order of monetary or fiscal manipulation. But the particular circumstances of the last two years have clearly acted to accelerate the inflationary trend. With the overall price level rising at a 10 per cent annual rate, with food prices rising more than twice as fast and with the general expectation that prices will continue to rise as fast if not faster, labour unions were no longer to be satisfied with the customary 5-to-10-per-cent pay concession. Impelled by anticipations of continuing inflation, by an awareness of the ground they had already lost in the last year and by an anxiety not to be 'outbid' by the claims of rival unions, wage demands are now of the order of between 20 and 30 per cent. Thus the tide of wage expectations is rising at a rate that must soon swamp the dykes hastily erected by the last government's income policy.

The 'pay pause' arising from the government's prices and incomes policy hardly helped matters. The Phase One 'freeze' (from November 1972 to March 1973) was short enough to be tolerated. The following six months of Phase Two (which permitted up to £1-a-week plus 4 per cent) was borne with, but under protest. The ill-fated Phase Three, which ineptly gives hostages to fortune by allowing a 40-pence increase for every percentage point above a further 7-per-cent rise in the cost of living index (which crucial figure we shall soon realise), was vigorously rejected by a number of powerful unions. In retrospect, the only certain effect of the Heath government's Income Policy — apart from a short truce on the wages front — was once more to rivet the attention of every occupational group in the country on its own pay position, both in relation to the cost of living and in relation to the pay of other occupational groups.

Exhortation in the circumstances is ineffective. Ministers have repeatedly declared that pay increases in excess of productivity increases can only raise prices further. For the economy as a whole, the exercise is not only futile but wasteful of energy. Yet, though true for 'the economy as a whole', it is not true for each particular segment of it. If the widget-makers union receives a pay increase in excess of the average, then it does indeed improve its position in real terms and in the general pay-structure, notwithstanding the consequent rise in widget prices. The widget-makers union know this. So does every other union. The appeal to enlightened self-interest persuades no one.

As for considerations of equity, at any time in modern history a consensus on a fair wage structure for industry would have been difficult to secure and difficult to implement. With the accent today largely on improving one's own union position relative to that of other unions, the notion of some hypothetical structure of wages acceptable to the trade-union movement as a whole is chimerical. An incomes policy predicated on the belief that there is such an animal — or that it can be brought into being by a concerted effort involving labour, management and government — is doomed to failure.

Finally, even if by some miracle agreement could be reached on the magnitude of ten thousand pay-differentials, and if (by some further miracle) the resulting pay structure were to coincide with the requirements of an efficient market, any future alteration of supply conditions, any technical innovation, any change in the pattern of demand, would dislodge this coincidence. If the resulting conflict between the market pay-structure and the original 'equit-able' pay-structure were politically resolved in favour of the latter, the consequence would be a redundancy of labour in some industries and a shortage of labour in others, and/or a mounting surplus of some goods and increasing shortage of others. Thus, a 'Relativities Board' that did not manage continually to re-align itself (under one formula or another) with the emerging patter of wants, as revealed by the market, could avoid similar wastes only if it were supple-mented by legislation charged with the overall direction of labour and capital.

THE APPEAL TO PATRIOTISM

In the last resort, as we know, there is always the appeal to patriotism. When the nation faces a common peril, factional interests must be swept aside. Such an appeal depends obviously on the public's perception of the danger that allegedly threatens it, and the sad truth is that today all government utterances on the gravity of a crisis are taken by the British public with more than a grain of salt. Were the public persuaded, however, of a real danger, its response would indeed depend on the extent of its patriot-ism. An appeal to all citizens to sink their differences and to make a sacrifice for the common good might have elicited some response before the last war. It is unlikely to do so today.

The last war came as near as can reasonably be expected in modern times to welding a country into a nation. Having stood alone for over a year, defying the might of the Wehrmacht, Britain emerged from the ordeal exhausted but unbroken, and with a new sense of national pride. Her perseverance and determination during that dark hour commanded the respect of all the Allied nations.

The spirit with which she emerged from the long-drawn conflict was an intangible asset, but an invaluable one. Wise statesmanship would have sought to shore it up against the disintegrative tide of the new affluence. But wise statesmanship has been in short supply for some time. The policies followed by successive governments could not have been better calculated to undermine this new-found national pride and self-confidence. Three episodes are illustrative: Commonwealth immigration, the legend of the 'English Disease', and the campaign surrounding Britain's entry into the EEC. A long word on each.

(1) Commonwealth Immigration. In the mid-1950s, immigration from Britain's ex-empire and -colonies mainly of unskilled workers and their families seeking employment and high wages in these (by any international standard) already crowded islands, began to build up. On some fundamental moral principle, perhaps, no hindrance to man's settling anywhere in the world can be justified. On such a principle, there can be no more objection to 200 millions settling in Britain than 2 millions. But if one's morality is more parochial, to the extent at least of evincing a concern about the impact of large-scale immigration of particular peoples on the welfare, the character and the political future of one's own countrymen, there is a case to be argued and a policy to be determined.

In the event, however, our enlightened rulers found nothing to argue about. Britain had long had a traditional open-door policy — which worked well enough so long as those who wished to pass through the open door (if we exclude our immediate neighbours, the Irish) never numbered more than a few thousand a year. Now that the stream of humanity coming through the still open door looked about to take on the dimensions of a torrent, second thoughts were called for.

As in so many critical issues since the war, however, the British people were just not consulted. Nor was this the last time a momentous decision was to be taken blithely on their behalf by enlightened governments with the connivance or support of the greater part of the press. Anyone who openly opposed this growing influx of migrants, indeed anyone who questioned it, was dismissed as a 'racist'. The prevailing liberal conscience apparently could discern no

more in the government's permissive policy than enlightened economic self-interest, a view illustrated by Mr R.A.
Butler's assertion (as late as 1961) that we in this country
needed the immigrants for the labour they provided.

To put it mildly, this was bad economics. For a general
shortage of labour, a general shortage of capital, a
general shortage of goods, indeed a general shortage of
everything but money, are the familiar symptoms of a
chronic inflation, and one that had afflicted Britain for a
decade. China, with about 400 million workers, could
just as well be made to generate a 'labour shortage' if its
government also failed persistently to curb aggregate
excess demand. In the event, the government made a
virtue of its incompetence to control the upward drift in
prices by conveying the impression that mass Commonwealth immigration was a welcome bonus to the domestic
labour market and was an essential plank in its economic
policy.

However, unlike the import of goods, the 'import' of
labour — and mostly unskilled labour at that — had two
adverse short-run effects in the existing economic circumstances. The consequent demand for additional industrial
and social capital, both to equip and to accommodate the
immigrants, was large enough to aggravate the excess
aggregate demand and so to contribute to the existing
inflation, while their import requirements served to worsen
the balance of payments. In the longer run, the most likely
effect of large-scale immigration of unskilled labour into
Britain is that of exerting a downward pressure on the
rising trend in real wages, and also of raising rents and
profits relative to wages.

Such economic consequences of large-scale immigration
into Britain are, however, only ancillary to the political
argument. They are illustrative of the delusions of the mid-
twentieth-century liberal mind, guided, as it has been since
the last war, more by dogmatic beliefs than by pragmatic
considerations. By 1962, when popular resentment could
no longer be ignored, the gates were officially closed, or
nearly so, and within were at least one million new
Commonwealth citizens. Today, augmented by net repro-

duction and by an unknown number of illegal immigrants, the figure of two million is more plausible.

Of course, we have had immigrants since the Norman invasion, and over time we have absorbed them and survived. And I would be the last to deny that fifty thousand or a hundred thousand of the new immigrants could have been assimilated in the fullness of time, and no one made much the worse for it. But a million or two of such immigrants is quite a different matter. For the first time in our long history we have become a multi-racial society. One can rejoice at the event or one can regret it. What one cannot do, with any pretence at honesty, is to act as if it does not signify — which is, of course, the official attitude.

As I remarked above, this extraordinary decision 'to go multi-racial' was never debated by the public at large. It was never even debated in Parliament. We simply blundered overnight, so to speak, into a multi-racial society that is also a 'multi-coloured' society, so adding to our existing social problems the incipient resentments, recriminations and all the pangs and tribulations that such a transformation entails — and out of which, as a matter of course, a number of enlightened liberals now make a passable living.

Political energy and economic resources have now to be expended in the endeavour to contain racial antagonisms on both sides, and to absorb these new citizens into the economy and, it is to be hoped, into the life of the country. If illegal immigration can be held down (a very big *if*), we may within the next fifty years or so have successfully integrated them into our society, if it is by then still in existence. But for the foreseeable future, the risks and disabilities of a new multi-racial society have to be borne with.

In the meantime, the idea of the British as a people is in the crucible. The ordinary man can no longer feel that this country is his country in the same way as before. And the allegiance of a sizable proportion of the population can no longer be taken for granted. For the immigrants do not yet share with us a common historical memory, much less a common pride in our past. Such mundane facts, added to the scepticism and disbelief bred of the New Affluence, must contribute to the erosion of those myths of 'kith and kin' which, though expendable enough for the truly detached intellectual, are the sources of inspiration that in moments of common danger bring citizens together ready and eager to make sacrifices.

(2) The 'English Disease'.

As already indicated, the central and unrelieved preoccupation of governments since the Second World War has been with the furtherance of economic growth. Elsewhere[6] I have sought to show that, for the wealthier countries at least, there is no longer any presumption that rising per-capita outputs enhance social well-being. Indeed, the contrary effect is more likely. Here I confine myself to the effect on the character of the British people arising from the policies, attitudes and pronouncements of British governments and the supporting Establishment once they have thrown themselves in abandon at the feet of the new golden calf. While repeated appeals to self-interest went part of the way to corrupt the good sense of the British, an unwitting but nonetheless insidious form of propaganda, supplemented by the visible scrapping of part of their heritage, went far to dissipate their confidence in themselves as a nation.

Once the GNP figure had become universally established as the measure of national achievement, and the Growth Rate accepted as the index of national virtue, the British people were to be represented by successive governments, by industrialists, journalists and technocrats — in fact all who fondly prided themselves on being in alliance with the Future — as the laggards of the New Europe. The laxity and smugness of the British were a theme of universal denigration. Newspaper editorials, radio commentary, lectures, tracts and sermons all waxed eloquent at some point on the topic of the 'English disease', and, when not facetious, spoke darkly of our impending eclipse by other more 'thrustful' countries. Sport it was to bemoan our 'lamentable growth performance' and to depict us as an effete power, lost without old empire and new purpose, growing in upon ourselves or declining into an amiable backwater of history, a sad and slightly ridiculous spectacle to those alert and go-ahead Europeans across the Channel. And such is the power of reiteration that by 1970, with all the modern paraphernalia of prosperity blatantly in evidence, cluttering up our homes and cluttering up our streets, half the house-wives of Britain, even those who couldn't tell a growth index from a prison record, had begun to worry about 'Britain's economic survival'.

By then, every facet of our national life, save the economic, had faded into insignificance. The British contribution to science and literature, to drama and ballet; Britain's unparalleled institutions, its BBC, its police force, its law courts, its university system; the political genius of the British people, the humaneness of their society, the prevailing climate of moderation and good sense — these inestimable national assets, all the product of a complex historical process, were just not agenda in the new economic assessment of the worth of a nation.

As early as 1960 the people of this country were being solemnly assured that only entry into the EEC could save them from virtual extinction. There they would drink reviving waters; there they would regain their strength and assume a leading role in the affairs of a new and powerful union. Every metaphor in the index, from the tonic effects of cold showers to the beckonings of manifest destiny, was enlisted in order to impress upon the ordinary citizen the imperative of merging his country's economic and political future with those of the Six.

The currency conversion came in 1971. The case for it in terms of economic efficiency alone is doubtful. Indeed, it is more than doubtful, since the changeover to a decimal currency (in which one new penny was equal 2·4 old pennies) has the predictable effect of giving a perceptible fillip to the upward drift of prices. Yet economic efficiency is but one consideration. There are others, seemingly less tangible but no less potent, of sentiment, pride and custom. Pounds, shillings and pence are not merely convenient units of account and currency. They are also an essential part of John Bull's accoutrements, an extension of Britain's personality. Our national system of weights and measures,

our pints and yards, our acres and fathoms, which are now
to be thrown into limbo as so much jetsam, are also part of
our Anglo-Saxon heritage. They ring familiar to our ears as
church bells. They are resonant with centuries of British
history. They are part of our language and our literature.
And in a world in which familiar landmarks are vanishing,
in which, as a result of rapid world communication and
mass tourism, differences in accent and architecture, differences in character and custom, are everywhere being
ironed out, there is much to be said for holding on ten-
aciously to these manifestations of a national persona. But,
on yet another issue of deep national concern, the government made no pretence even of consulting the feelings of
the British people.

In between bouts of excoriating the nation for its wilful
slackness, governments have also found time to wheedle it
for electoral reasons. Apparently, we had 'never had it so
good', and there was always more mod-cons gadgetry on
the way. For, after all, we were becoming richer — though,
of course, not nearly so fast as we should like.

Admittedly, it can be argued that recurrent appeals to
greed, to ambition and to self-seeking could make little
difference in view of the strong secular forces operating to
foster opportunism. Yet whatever difference it could make
was thrown into the same scale as those secular forces,
adding its weight to them.

(3) Britain's Debut into the Common Market.
The government's decision in 1972 to make Britain a
member of the EEC was more than a snub to the manifest
lingerings of national sentiment in the country, which it
regarded simply as an anachronism. It was the culmination
of a policy pursued by successive governments since 1960,
one marked by an increasing readiness effectively to
repudiate a rich and unique patrimony in order to be seen
bravely facing 'the winds of change' — which, it was confidently expected, would blow up our GNP a little faster.
For over a decade the heads of all three political parties
had been calmly contemplating an Act that would formally
set in motion a process the intent and culmination of which

was to expunge the identity and annul the sovereignty of the British people in exchange for a windy seat in this contrived and cumbersome Continental polity — though always with the telling proviso that 'the price' should be 'right'.

British governments knew perfectly well that membership in such a union implied eventually a surrender of sovereignty. The Treaty of Rome was explicit on this issue, and the founding fathers of the European Union advised us more than once that they were 'not in business, but in politics'. For all that, British pro-Marketeers put the stress of their propaganda on the supposed economic advantages. Admittedly, there would be some upward 'harmonisation' of food prices, and some contribution to be made to the common budget. But all this would be as nothing compared with the magnitude of those imponderable long-term benefits which, as it happened, began to recede into a mist of vagueness and verbiage as the moment drew closer. Indeed, on the very eve of our entry, Mr Heath's buoyant spirits were muted for a few minutes as, over the air, he cautioned the nation in effect not to be too impatient to redeem the promissory notes so lavishly distributed by the pro-Marketeers. Those 'immeasurable' long-term economic benefits, which had featured so large in the government's pro-Market propaganda,[7] might not, he now owned, be enjoyed in our own lifetime, perhaps not even in our children's lifetime, but in our children's children's lifetime.

When in the early 1970's the issue of sovereignty was becoming more difficult to evade, two tactics were employed. One was to deny that our sovereignty, in any real sense, would be impaired by entering the EEC. The other was to assert that there was, in any case, no meaningful sovereignty left to impair, either on the ground that a Britain unconjoined with the EEC could not be expected to survive as an economically viable entity or, more generally, on the grounds that sovereignty in the modern world was after all no more than a fiction (a proposition which, strangely enough, was supposed to follow from the premise that any nation's sovereign powers were subject to restraints in a world of sovereign states).

A year of membership in this bureaucratic European Club, with its endless manoeuvre and intrigue, has at least had the salutary effect of making two things crystal clear: first, that the sovereignty of Parliament is indeed being trimmed around the edges (as was confirmed in the report of the recent parliamentary committee set up in response to protests about the indigestible flow of regulations and directives emanating from the Brussels Commission); second, that those loudly heralded long-run economic benefits are after all, as so many of us had in any case suspected, to be reaped only in the 'Keynesian long run' — that is, 'when we are all dead'.

Yet, however we rate the economic and political consequences, the fact remains that on a constitutional issue of momentous consequence for the nation, the government chose to ignore the widespread public antipathy and to avail itself of a small parliamentary majority to haul the country into the Market. For so unprecedented and apparently irrevocable a constitutional innovation, one that would for the first time in Britain's long history merge her institutions and her sovereignty into a wider political entity, surely nothing less than an overwhelming approval of the British people would have sufficed; at least, say, a two-thirds majority in Parliament and in the country at large. In the event, the government's decision failed to elicit the support even of half the country, a fact that apparently caused it no distress whatsoever since it chose to interpret its election to office as conferring on it a mandate 'to lead the nation', even if (or rather especially if) on this occasion it meant 'dragging the country screaming into the twentieth century'.

So Mr Heath wrote himself, or rather entangled himself, into history and secured for the ungrateful British that much-coveted prize, 'a voice in the Council of Europe'. Initially, of course, it was only Mr Heath's authentic voice, large and leaden with the clichés of statesmanship. And though it sounds loud enough at home, on the Continent it was invariably topped by M. Pompidou's louder voice.

Ironically enough, it was Mr Heath who, having publicly and joyfully severed the trappings of nationality at the beginning of 1973, was then to appeal to recalcitrant labour unions, at a time of crisis, towards the end of the year, in the name of 'national unity'.

THE EMERGING PATTERN

Let me, in conclusion, bring together the pieces that make up the broad picture, the larger pieces exhibited above and some of the smaller pieces that can now be fitted in without cluttering it with too much detail.

Put in its bluntest terms, the thesis I argue is that the chief causes of contemporary inflations are linked closely with the current stage of economic growth. The primary fact is that the post-war world is convulsed by a dangerous virus commonly referred to as 'the revolution of rising expectations'. Among the poorer countries, the growing discontent is easily translated into disaffection which, where it has not been repressed by virtual dictatorship, has created social and political instability. In the wealthier non-communist countries, however, this chronic dissatisfaction and restlessness have themselves influenced monetary and fiscal laxity, and it has brought them that much closer to self-sustaining inflation.

Following the post-war reconstruction period, from 1945 to about 1950, the inflationary impulse arose directly from the growing optimism shared both by ordinary people and by businessmen. With a 'live today, pay tomorrow' spirit in the air, expenditures on consumption and investment goods remained high. They were supplemented — in response to widespread expectations of more extensive welfare services by the state — by increasing outlays on the public sector of the economy that were, in any case, a far larger proportion of national expenditure than they were before the Second World War. Given the high level of employment, which (it was popularly thought) governments were able and, therefore, politically obliged to maintain, given also the psychology of a new generation that had never lived through an economic slump or even through a period of falling prices, the resultant tendency (up to 1970) to slip into overall excess expenditure and rising inflation is not surprising.

This milder form of inflation in the West may now be regarded only as a first phase. It could, perhaps, have been controlled for a time by conventional economic remedies, had they been promptly and competently applied by governments less eager than in fact they were both to whet and to appease the affluent citizen's already enlarged appetites. But the mushroom growth of expectations in the West, at least, has come to embrace a new feature. As a result, inflation today is entering a new and more virulent phase.

Although universal impatience with existing material standards accompanied by expectations of more, ever more, tends to breed inflation in so far as it issues in excessive expenditure by consumers, by governments and businessmen, there is now more to it than that. There is a new development arising from the technological aspects of economic growth. Industrial advances that increase the size of the optimal plant or public utility act inevitably to increase the vulnerability of population centres that depend upon them. At the same time, the post-war spread of news media has enabled organized labour to realise more quickly the power it can wield by depriving the community at large of essential services or by exposing it to inconvenience or risk.

Owing to our recent familiarity with this form of collective blackmail, its significance has not been fully appreciated by the liberal economist. Economic opportunism has been valued by the liberal or *laissez-faire* economist as the animus that inspires the 'invisible hand'. To the growth economist in particular, habitual discontent is positively esteemed as being the mainspring of economic progress. Ignoring the broader social implications of such a presumption, its corollaries are valid enough provided the diffusion of discontent and opportunism expresses itself in personal efforts as self-betterment through increased exertion and enterprise. If instead this ethos-embedded discontent finds vent in collective action, in agitating for a bigger share of the annual cornucopia of goodies, it helps neither to animate the invisible hand nor to promote economic progress. It promotes only inflation — all the more so, as it is seen by all to be effective, and seen by all to be resistant to the economist's conventional fiscal and monetary instruments.

We may plausibly conclude that there are turbulent times ahead for the West. For we seem to have reached a stage where we have to make a political choice between price stability and maintaining traditional freedoms to the extent, at least, of leaving intact the existing power of trade unions and shop stewards. Certainly, price stability, high employment and free collective bargaining, are no longer mutually compatible.

To fill in the picture, these growth-produced developments have to be supplemented by others of a less tangible nature.

The concomitant decline of patriotic sentiment, of civil pride, of *civitas*, means that there is today no strong countervailing force which the state can invoke in times of crisis. This tendency, too, is an unavoidable by-product of economic progress. For this decline of patriotism, along with the erosion of moral consensus and religious faith, is the counterpart of the spread of scepticism and disbelief attributable to the growth of secular knowledge and education. The most obscure citizen today, tuning in to his favourite programme, hears once-sacred beliefs and moral presuppositions subjected to repeated probing, dissection and doubt.

To these morally debilitating developments may be added some auxiliary, possibly transitory, but nonetheless growth-induced factors. One is the new pop culture, which emerged partly in response to an affluence-begotten youth market with a commercial emphasis on excitement, on stylised violence and carnality; a pop culture sporting a permissive 'own thing' ethic that is antithetic to traditional values and, more generally, to social order. Thus the idealism of the young finds little outlet in any form of patriotic feelings — it is frittered away in a vague universalism, with passions reserved only for group or gang loyalties, for 'them and us', for sporadic movements and ephemeral causes and cults.[8]

The case of the UK, however, has an additional special
interest in so far as the Establishment there, ably represented by successive post-war governments in their fatuous
and fulsome worship of economic growth, went out of its
way to undermine the self-respect and confidence of the
British people, to extinguish their sense of national identity
and to cut them off from their history by tearing up the
emblems and regalia of their past — all in the cheerless
cause and under the tawdry banner of economic efficiency.

A dispiriting parade of shuffling ministers sniffing wearily
in the winds of change for economic clues to the shape of
the future have persistently sought to reduce their
countrymen to economic men pure and simple, economic
men caring for naught but the size of their pay packets —
and the size of everyone else's. The extent of their success
in this sorry endeavour, abetted as they were in any case by
complex forces unleashed by economic growth, is today
also a measure of the extent of their failure to control this
new and more dangerous phase of inflation.

NOTES

1. A Keynesian-based stability policy does not rule out the deliberate
    creation of large budget-deficits if, for any reason, aggregate
    investment (plus excess exports over imports) tends to fall below
    full-employment saving. But although the economic situation in the
    1930s might be summarised in these terms, that prevailing in the
    post-war period was for the most part the reverse of this and, on a
    Keynesian view, would have warranted a policy of budget surpluses
    and high interest rates. True, nominal interest rates are today the
    highest in living memory. But once allowance is made for the
    anticipated rise in the price level, which is certainly well over 10 per
    cent per annum, the 'real' return on any government bond *net* of tax
    is negative, and has been negative for many years.

2. This is obviously a simplified account in which professional incomes,
    pensions, profits and import prices are ignored. In so far as they are
    brought into the picture, total money income may rise less than
    workers' income. But the margin they can provide in limiting the
    price rise is operative only at the beginning of such a process.

3. The interested reader is referred to a study by E.J. Mishan and L.A. Dicks-Mireaux, 'Progressive Taxation in an Inflationary Economy', *American Economic Review*, September 1958.

4. The workers' growing tax awareness is discussed in some detail in an excellent booklet, *Do Trade Unions Cause Inflation?* by L. Jackson, J. Turner and W. Wilkinson, put out by the Department of Applied Economics, Cambridge (1972). Such is the extent of the tax deduction from wages that the authors suggest the unions could substantially increase the real earning of their members by negotiating for simultaneous reductions of prices and wages!

5. Brian Griffiths. 'Inflation: Causes, Consequences and Policies' appears in *Inflation: Economy and Society*, ed. by Lionel Robbins, Institute of Economic Affairs (1972).

6. For instance, in my *Encounter* article, 'To Grow or Not to Grow: What are the Issues?', May 1973.

7. House of Commons, June 14, 1971. *Sir Derek Walker-Smith (East Hertfordshire, Conservative)*: 'With regard to the so-called dynamic effects, will he [Mr John Davies] repeat in this House and to the country what he said with such admirable candour in his press conference in Stockholm to the effect that these so-called dynamic effects were not capable of measurement?'
   Mr John Davies (Secretary of State for Trade and Industry): 'I have never failed to say so. It is clear at this time that they are not capable of accurate forward assessment, but that they are powerful and will predominate, I have no doubt.' (Reported in *The Times*, 15 June 1971.)

8. The ebb of patriotic sentiment is hastened by the transformation of the physical environment itself in response to the more recent products of economic growth. For it is becoming harder for the British, the young in particular, to think affectionately of their country as an island home when the continual roar overhead suggests that it is more of a gigantic airstrip, a place of perpetual transit, a stopping-off point in the international tourists' itinerary.

PART II

INTRODUCTION

The myth that is the most painful to expose is the myth that economics, the most advanced of the social sciences, is on a par with the physical sciences. While I cast no aspersion at the beginning of my Chapter 4 on the intellectual integrity and sophistication of my fellow economists, and do not question their eagerness to discover new economic relationships and their readiness to measure them in circumstances of considerable difficulty, I do take the view that adherence to a valid methodology, in particular a willingness to subject theories to empirical tests, is not of itself a sufficient criterion. At any rate the fact remains that after some 200 years of cultivation, the harvest of reliable empirical propositions yielded by the subject is discouragingly meagre — a fact which is not likely to change over the future, for reasons given in that chapter.

It is more sensible, rather, to regard economics as being primarily a branch of applied logic, one through which we study the implications of individual and social choice, aided only, and occasionally, by the simplest empirical constructs. Conceived in this way, other economic myths may be uncovered.

For instance, business men and numbers of economists have sought to persuade the public that the growth of government activity not only threatens political freedom, which it may do, but that it necessarily reduces individual choice. The latter allegation, however, is far from self-evident, notwithstanding the excellent book by Milton and Rose Friedman, *Free to Choose* (1979).

As I suggest in Chapter 3, the disamenities of industrial overspill and of mass consumption and mobility continue to whittle away individual choice independent of the size of governments. And it is important to realise that this is true even where spillover effects are so corrected that resource allocation is as perfect as can reasonably be expected.

It is therefore not hard to show that if we extend our vision beyond the production of private or market goods to encompass environmental goods, a conclusion contrary to that held by businessmen and economists may be defended. Inasmuch as environmental goods are being valued more highly in the advanced industrialised economies, it is often the case that only government legislation and its creation of collective goods can extend the citizen's choice in significant ways.

Another belief, common among mainstream economists, is that in a world of finite deposits of material resources, no conservation policies are needed. Competitive markets of themselves can be depended upon to ensure that over time global consumption of the limited amount of any of these materials proceeds at an 'optimal' rate — or so, under familiar assumptions, runs the theory.

Under ideal conditions this would indeed be true for a population of given individuals, nobody dying and nobody being born. Once we introduce an indefinite number of future generations, the theory is false. It can be shown that the benefits and losses of generations yet unborn can *not* be converted, via any discount rate, to a net present value which can be vindicated by recourse to an acceptable economic criterion.

Finally, in Chapter 5, I touch again on a seemingly ineradicable belief current in all political parties, from the extreme Right to the extreme Left; namely, that the growth of GNP (or GDP) or net national income per capita is at least a rough index of the improvement over time of living standards. But this persistent belief is no longer plausible, neither with respect to magnitude or direction, when account is taken of the increasing proportion of aggregate economic activity that is devoted to the regrettable though necessary task of restoring and maintaining standards of community service, of security, of health, of amenity and of environmental protection in an increasingly complex and vulnerable civilization. There are, of course, other reasons for scepticism, some

of which appear in that chapter and others elsewhere in
this volume.

3 The Limits to Freedom of Choice

The *leitmotif* of Professor Friedman's book, *Free to Choose,* [1] and its implied criterion of economic virtue, is — as suggested by the title — the extent of the choice among goods that is available to the individual, and not efficient allocation as conventionally understood by economists.

Although the growth in economic prosperity is regarded by Friedman as a consequence, largely, of freedom of economic choice — a term which embraces freedom of private enterprise — his powerful critique of the post-war expansion of the government sector of the economy, maintained by a hydra-headed bureaucracy, is founded in the main upon the criterion of individual choice. In contrast, the post-war literature on externalities or, more generally, the literature on what is commonly called 'market failure' (initially developed in Pigou's classic *Economics of Welfare*, although the germ of the idea harks back to Dupuit, 1840) has evolved by reference almost entirely to the criterion of resource allocation. Moreover, the new realism brought to bear on the externalities literature (dating from Coase's long-winded paper of 1960),[2] which invokes the concepts of property rights, transaction costs and the like — the detailed implications of which have used up so many pages of the *Journal of Law and Economics* — serves also to emphasize the concentration of economists on the allocative aspects that are seemingly the very pith and marrow of all writings on Welfare Economics whether 'Old' or 'New'.

Although in any particular example a measure of net social benefit in moving from an existing situation that is already allocatively optimal to an alternative situation that, in addition, extends individual choice, is at least conceptually calculable, a general ranking on some scale of social welfare of these two distinct criteria — that of resource allocation and that of individual choice — has to remain a matter of broad judgment, one that is not made easier by the realization that the two criteria are nonetheless related in the way a hypothetical economic improvement of society is related to an actual one.

A ranking of these two criteria is not, however, necessary for the purpose of this essay, which restricts itself to subjecting the more familiar propositions of the externality literature to the new criterion, that of individual choice; more particularly, to re-examining the various arrangements that — within a partial economic context — satisfy allocative norms in order to determine whether, and to what extent, they also satisfy the freedom-to-choose requirement.[3]

I

First, a word about the relation between individual choice and individual welfare. The normative economist's view, from which I do not depart here, conceives of the individual's area of choice, or of his 'choice set', as enlarged when *ceteris paribus* (which clause is deemed to hold constant his tastes, all other prices and all non-economic variables) there is a fall in one or more product prices or a rise in one or more of his factor prices, or else when a new good becomes available or a new opportunity for his factors. Only in a limiting case will the welfare of the individual not rise in these circumstances, so that in general such an expansion of the individual's choice set is equated with an increase in his welfare.

The relation is of course symmetric. Under the same *ceteris paribus* clause, a rise in product prices or a fall in the individual's factor prices, or a withdrawal of previously available goods or factor opportunities, constitutes a contraction of the individual's choice set and a reduction of his welfare. More generally, of course, the

individual will be faced over time with opposite movements of both factor and product prices, with both the
introduction of new opportunities and the withdrawal of
existing ones, so that his choice set will be expanded in
some respects and restricted in others, as a result of
which his welfare will, on balance, increase or decrease.
Nevertheless, when he is free to choose some new set, we
may assume that he may be better off but not worse off.
If, in contrast, he is not free to reject the new set, he may
well become worse off.

Since the above paragraphs have references only to
goods resulting from the operation of the economy, some
additional remarks may be helpful in involving the notion
of political choice also. A person who abides by society's
constitution may disapprove or vote against a particular
measure, notwithstanding which he may be said, constitutionally speaking, to accept — and, therefore, in a
sense to 'choose' — the measure even though, politically
speaking, he rejects it. If the distinction is granted, it
follows that Friedman's thesis is confined to the individual regarded simply as a political and economic animal.
Consider him, then, provisionally as such a political
animal voting for a particular measure; say, one requiring
the government to supply one or more goods to some or
all members of society. It may indeed appear better to
many or the majority of individuals to receive goods from
the government on more advantageous terms (in the
limiting case receiving the goods free of charge) than
having them currently available on the market. The
apparent free choice of this segment of the voters is for
public-sector provision of the goods in question. There
will, however, also be a minority of voters, politico-
economic men, who are made worse off financially, some
or all of whom will believe they are injured by this
legislation. Describing the situation in this way invites a
conclusion that the expansion of the government sector
entailed by this legislation reflects a free choice of some
individuals though not of others.

What Friedman and others are at pains to point out,
however, is that examples couched in such terms fail to

separate two aspects: the transfer aspect and the receipt-of-cash-or-kind aspect. Although each individual in a particular income bracket may agree to a legislative proposal that transfers x dollars from his income for the benefit of others *provided* all others similarly circumstanced are obliged to do the same, this redistribution of purchasing power does not involve coercion, even though — as Garrett Hardin (1977) puts it — it is 'mutual coercion mutually agreed upon'.[4] Such coercion is consistent with many of the donors being better off, as well as with the recipients all being better off. The point of Friedman's economic argument is, however, that once the proceeds of the transfer are used to provide members of society directly with goods, then each of them foregoes effective choice in one important respect. For compared with the alternative of receiving the cash equivalent of the value of those goods he is entitled to, each individual will, in general, be worse off.

Abstracting, then from the distributional aspects of the public provision of goods, it follows that irrespective of whether any individual is, on balance, better or worse off, he is certainly not so well off as he would be if, instead, he could have the money equivalent of the goods publicly provided and use the money to choose any amounts of any goods he pleases at the market prices. In consequence of the government's foreclosure of this option, individuals have to forego this preferred choice.

II

Three proposals will, if accepted, simplify the task of exposition.
(1) We refrain from taking issue with the standard assumption that the individual prefers more to less, even though it is now recognized that the variety of brands and models on the market will, once they exceed a certain number, begin to drag on the individual's patience. The question of whether there are any dependable mechanisms within a competitive private

sector of the economy that tend to produce an optimal variety is an interesting one, though I shall not explore it here. Nor shall I examine the related question whether the structure of each item offered by the market is that which best meets the requirements of consumers; more specifically, the question whether a decomposition of some existing items (for example, the opportunity of buying components that enable a person to put together a refrigerator more suitable to his particular taste or purpose) and also, perhaps, whether a combination of items currently sold separately (for example, the opportunity of buying houses that are already fully decorated and furnished) might not extend the area of individual choice. Although such questions are topical enough, they may be neglected since their resolution is unlikely to affect the main force of Friedman's thesis.

(2) We agree to say that an externality has been 'internalized' either:

(a) when it has been accorded an accounting price within a business organization, or

(b) when it has been priced on the market, or

(c) when the scarce resource, ownership of which permits control of the externality in question, has an accounting or a market price.

A familiar example of (a) would be a merger of that imperishable up-stream polluting business with its unfortunate down-stream counterpart, as a result of which the effluent once suffered by the latter business is accorded an accounting price by the merger. An example of (b) would be the straw that is the by-product of grain production, which straw confers an external economy on the poorer peasants who gather it to make palliasses, a situation that continues until such time as the supply and demand for straw become large enough to justify the formation of a market in straw. An example of (c) begins with the scarce resource, agricultural land, say, which, when placed under private ownership

acquires either an accounting or a market price,
so providing the inducement necessary for producers to determine output by reference to
marginal labour cost — a schedule that takes
proper account of the externalities imposed by
the additional worker on the product of intra-
marginal workers.

(3) The third proposal is in fact a plea for licence to use
the word 'externality' in much the same way as pollution or congestion is used in ordinary parlance —
notwithstanding, that is, the arguments of economists
(Dahlman, 1979, being a recent example)[5] who favour
using the word only where, by reference to a comprehensive allocation criterion,[6] it remains uncorrected.
Thus, following their line of thought, what may initially be regarded as an externality is deemed to vanish
whenever the misallocation it might cause is corrected
in any of a number of ways — including bargaining
between the affected parties irrespective of which
holds the relevant property rights. Yet since I wish to
show, among other things, that for some economic
arrangements the allocative correction of an externality does not, of itself, preclude the continued
existence of a residual or even an optimal amount of
the substance identified with the externality, I cannot
comfortably adopt the definition of externality favoured
by them. Therefore, whatever the nature of the disamenity that is associated with the externaility in question,
I shall continue to refer to it as the externality so long as
any amount of it remains to inflict discomfort or damage
on one or more individuals.[7]

III

A package consists of a number of items, goods and/or
bads, some given amount of which has to be taken by the
individual who receives the package at a price that may
be positive, zero or negative. (The limiting case of a
package is, of course, a single item.)

An obvious distinction has to be made between a *voluntary* and an *involuntary* package. A voluntary package of goods and/or bads is one that the individual agrees to receive at a price — positive (a price he pays), zero (free) or negative (a price he receives). The acceptance of the voluntary package may unambiguously extend the individual's choice set as defined or else it may be ambiguous in this respect — extending it for some items, contracting it for others. Nonetheless, inasmuch as the individual voluntarily accepts the package on the terms offered, he is assumed to be made better off.

An involuntary package, on the other hand, is one that is imposed upon the individual at a price (positive, zero or negative), whether or not he would otherwise have accepted it. He cannot, therefore, be assumed to be made better off by receiving it. More specifically, the involuntary package received may arise either:

(1) From political activity, being imposed by the government. In such a case it takes the form of a transfer payment to or from the individual (which could be zero) along with the provision of goods and/or bads at prices that can be positive, negative or zero.[8]

(2) It may arise from economic activity, being imposed as an externality. In that case it takes the form of the availability of a good or a bad at a price along with one or more collective goods and/or bads.

Within the standard partial economic context, the introduction into the economy of a voluntary package confers on the community an actual Pareto improvement since no one is made worse off whereas those who choose to avail themselves of the offer are assumed to be made better off.

In contrast, the introduction of an involuntary package cannot be assumed to make anybody better off. Whether an individual welcomes the package or deplores it, he has no choice in the matter. Since some individuals may certainly be worse off, a Pareto improvement for society is *not* entailed by the introduction of an involuntary package.[9] And the fact that an individual may avail himself, although at some cost or inconvenience, of oppor-

tunities so as to reduce the consequent loss of welfare
initially suffered by having to bear the involuntary
package[10] does not of itself alter this conclusion.

In this latter connexion, then, it is hardly necessary to
add that the costs of movement and adjustment — both
pecuniary and psychological — cannot be assumed to be
zero; for in a hypothetical world, within which the movement and adjustments necessary to remove entirely the
initial 'diswelfare' associated with the involuntary package are costless, there can be no effective reduction of
any individual's choice: all bads to an individual, that is,
can be avoided at no cost. It would then follow that no
package or item produced by the market (even though it
generates externalities) can reduce an individual's welfare, and therefore that all new packages and items
necessarily confer Pareto improvements. In such a world,
therefore, the problem we are concerned with does not
arise.

IV

Prior to the exposition proper, a simply proposition
has to be borne in mind. If there are altogether n different items (in given quantities) available to the individual
in one package for a single sum y, and then these n items
are decomposed in any way into smaller packages, he will
at least be no worse off *always provided* that the aggregate of the prices of the new packages does not exceed
the sum of y. In general, the n different items can be
goods or bads or both, and the initial sum y can be
positive or negative. To illustrate with simple examples,
if the market offers the individual the choice only of a
package of two oranges and three apples for $1, then he
will be at least no worse off whatever the price set for a
single apple and for a single orange provided only that
the two prices are such that an expenditure of $1 will now
enable him to buy (at least) two oranges and three apples
— although he may well want to avail himself of the new
opportunity (of buying apples and oranges separately at

these prices) as to purchase them in proportions quite different from the original package of two oranges to three apples. In that case, the economist infers that the decomposition of the package confers on the individual a gain in welfare. The second example is that of a package consisting only of one good and one bad, say the right of an individual to occupy a specific house for $10,000 a year that, incidentally, exposes him to continuous traffic noise. He would be at least as well off if he were to be offered the identical kind of house *less* the traffic noise at a price in excess of $10,000 a year along with the opportunity to bear with some amount of traffic noise in return for some payment, or price, per unit of noise borne, *provided,* again, that the algebraic sum of the price he now pays for the house plus the amount of money he would receive for bearing the original amount of traffic noise at the price per unit would not exceed $10,000.

This proposition is, indeed, self-evident inasmuch as, whatever the separate prices set, the same sum y is (by the terms of the proposition) such as to enable him to buy the original package if he so chooses — although he may well avail himself of the separate prices to choose a combination of items different from that of the original package. By reference to the conventions used in connexion with revealed preference, we may say that, in general, such decomposition of a voluntary package makes the individual better off.

V

We turn now to the effect on individual choice of the incidence of externalities under two main headings: case A, those externalities that are *internal* to the activity in question, and (in sect. VII) case B, those that, in contrast, are *external* to that activity.[11] The simple model to keep in mind is that most commonly used within a partial context in which the price-demand curve for a good x is usefully conceived as the consumers' marginal valuation curve for x, and the correction for externalities, if any, takes the form of some adjustment of the corresponding supply curve of x — the optimal output of x being one for which price is equal to marginal *social* cost. An alternative and seemingly less restrictive model in which the physical units are not goods but units of pollution — the optimal level of pollution being that for which the marginal social benefit of pollution-removal is equal to its marginal resource cost[12] — is more appropriate for the case B, of externalities external to the activity. Its adoption for both cases A and B, however, would add complexity to some parts of the exposition without adding any significant modification to the conclusion.

Case A: Let us consider first those externalities internal to the activity that are internalized as defined earlier, and which externalities (in the sense, I remind the reader, of unwanted disamenity), moreover, are not actually experienced by individuals.

Those externalities arising in efficient agricultural production come under this category. This (1) given the equality of some privately owned land that is specific to corn growing, there is a level of corn output after which diminishing returns set in; that is to say, each additional labourer employed on this land inflicts external diseconomies internal to the corn growing activity itself. In consequence, each additional labourer reduces the average product of labour.

This effect on the product of intra-marginal labour is properly allowed for by the producer's being guided in his employment of labour by reference to the *marginal* product curve of labour. Assuming the wage rate is fixed, this procedure translates into that of taking the marginal labour cost as the relevant cost curve in determining the output of corn.[13]

All this is elementary enough but needs to be restated for the purpose of analogies to be made. This particular case, however, is that in which the externality is already internalized inasmuch as the land — the resource whose scarcity results in the externality in question — is either priced on the market or, being owned by the producer, is assigned an accounting price by him.

A formally analogous example is (2) that of sea fishing. At present, any particular fishing grounds are unpriced. The external diseconomies internal to the fishing activity (which is reflected in the diminishing average returns that accrue to it) are not internalized as they are in efficient agriculture and, as a result, there is 'over-fishing'.[14] If, however, the fishing grounds were allocated to a person or corporation as an exclusive property, they would command a market or accounting price. The externality would thus be internalized.

VI

We have now to consider two other familiar examples in which external diseconomies internal to the activity are or may be internalized. These two cases are formally identical with those above with respect to allocation, but are different with respect to individual choice.

First, let us look at (3) Knight's example of a new highway which is placed under private ownership. The eventual traffic congestion on this new highway can be presented as a curve of rising average cost per journey, each additional vehicle inflicting external diseconomies in the shape of congestion costs on the intra-marginal traffic. The owner of this new highway is assumed to choose that volume of traffic which maximizes his revenue, a task that may be achieved by taking a curve that is marginal to the rising average cost curve and choosing the volume of traffic for which this marginal cost is equal to the marginal valuation of the journey.[15]

The second example is that of (4) a new industrial town aptly dubbed Smoke City. We are to assume that the industries located within it generate an unchanged amount of smoke. Because of the smoke, each specific type of labour will have to be paid a premium above the prevailing market rate, a premium that may have to increase with the amount of labour needed by Smoke City.[16] If so, the market smoke-premium can be taken to equal the value of the smoke-externality as experienced

by the marginal worker, each intra-marginal worker
receiving a rent equal to that market smoke-premium less
the minimum premium that would induce him to bear the
smoke.

With the usual proviso about competition, the market
in each of these two cases (3) and (4) is working efficiently and effectively internalizing the externality. But there
is one difference between these two cases and those of
(1) and (2). In the two cases (3) and (4) — that of the
new highway and that of Smoke City — the individuals
are offered a package, whereas in the original cases (1)
and (2) they are not.

On my adopted definition there is still some externality
even if, in each of the four cases, an optimal amount of
the good (and of the externality) is being produced. But
notice that in cases (3) and (4) the individual who
chooses to engage in the activity continues to experience
the external diseconomy along with the experience of the
good itself. In case (3) the motorist who pays the toll for
use of the new highway, a good in its own right, has to
continue to bear with some congestion (a bad), even
though the economist may assure him that this congestion
is optimal. On balance, of course, he himself chooses this
package of good-*cum*-bad, the availability of which may
properly be said to raise his level of welfare. According
to our decomposition proposition, of course, he would be
still better off if this package could be decomposed, and
the highway service and the congestion be marketed
separately — although, in the nature of things, this may
be impossible to arrange.

Like remarks apply to case (4). The workers who elect to
move to Smoke City accept a voluntary package containing
two bads, work plus smoke, in exchange for the price the
market will pay. A Pareto improvement is clearly implied
by the availability of this package, although, once again
workers could be made still better off if each of the bad
were available at its own market price.

In case (1) in contrast to the above cases (3) and (4)
the externality internal to the corn-growing activity
which has been internalized in consequence of a marke

price being set for the scarce corn-growing land, is *not* directly experienced by the individuals involved. No disamenity is experienced by the workers themselves from the diminishing average product that ensues as employment increases. The worker does not, therefore, have the choice of a package of two bads as in case (4); for here the externality that produces a reduction in the average product of labour is borne entirely by consumers in the shape of a higher price of corn.[17]

As for case (2), once fishing grounds are made exclusive property and command a price or rent, the outcome is in every respect like that of case (1). For, again, the externality is not directly experienced by the fishermen: they, too, are not faced with a package of two bads or else of a good-*cum*-bad — as in cases (4) and (3), respectively. The effect of the external diseconomy internal to sea fishing is borne by the consumers in the form of a higher price of fish.

Consider, however, a small modification of case (3), which we call case (3'), in which the owner of the highway uses it only for his own fleet of trucks. This new (3') case is now identical in every respect with cases (1) and (2). The users of the highway are now all truck-drivers in the pay of the highway owner. At the market rate for the job, the prevalence of an optimal level of congestion does not affect the truck-driver personally any more than it affects the fisherman or the agricultural worker. The external diseconomy internal to the operation of the highway is borne entirely by the consumer through higher freight charges.

It may *not* be concluded, however, that for all cases of externalities internal to the activity that are, in the event, internalized through prices, choice is extended to individuals even if the choice comes in package form. This statement is borne out by considering a case (4') that differs from (4) only in that workers *already* dwell in what is soon to become Smoke City. As the event takes place, workers may be observed to continue to work here at the unchanged market rate, even though they now suffer from the smoke. All that may be inferred from this observation is that, on balance, the workers elect to bear with this new bad rather than incur the costs of moving to a less smoky location.

Inasmuch as, from an initial position of smokeless air, smoke is now imposed upon the worker without his consent, he cannot be said to choose it along with his work in a voluntary package deal as in case (4). We may continue to refer to the two bads in case (4') as a package, but clearly it is not a voluntary package. It is no longer correct, therefore, to regard this package, an involuntary one, as of the worker's free choice. Certainly, there is no presumption of an actual Pareto improvement.

Put otherwise, the unanticipated introduction only of the externality smoke and nothing else reduces the individual's area of choice, since a bad that is imposed upon a person is tantamount to the reduction of a good that was previously available to him.[18]

VII

Case B: The picture is quite different when we turn to the B category of externalities, those that are external to the activity. Under the provisional assumption of zero welfare and zero transactions costs, it is a matter of indifference for an allocation criterion whether the corn farmer or the rancher, in the well-known Coase example,[19] was first to establish his business and whether the farmer has to pay the rancher or the rancher the farmer. Not so, however, for a choice criterion.

If the farmer is in business first, and the rancher then occupies the adjacent land, then, prior to bargaining, a bad is definitely imposed upon the farmer. His choice set is reduced. The fact that he is willing to pay the rancher certain sums to induce him to take measures to prevent his cattle straying onto the farm land, in the endeavour to reduce the extent of the losses he must in any event suffer, may be regarded as costs incurred simply in mitigating the impact of this misfortune. But it does not alter the conclusion.

The man whose splendid view of the mountains is obstructed, though quite legally, by the building of a new residence is similarly afflicted. Indeed, as the world fills up and mobility increases, we may anticipate a reduction in individual choice from externalities that turn on location.[20]

Conclusions about choices are, of course, much more important when we turn from the two-person case to those externalities that are inflicted upon the public at large. Provided the amount is positive, the optimal level of some specific effluent resulting, say, from the imposition of an optimal effluent tax, does indeed continue to inflict damage on individuals without their consent and without compensation. As a result, they suffer a reduction in their welfare.

To illustrate, effluent can be defined to include noise; more specifically, say, aircraft noise. But though this aircraft noise may be reduced to an optimum with respect to all relevant characteristics, it may yet be consistent with much nuisance and damage.[21] The committed growth-man is prone to argue that the noise and any other incidental disamenities and hazards suffered are the price of progress — the relevant bit of progress being the opportunity to travel by air, an opportunity denied to all previous generations. However, this does not solve the problem. The welfare state also provides men with historically unprecedented opportunities; for example, in Britain, the availability to all of 'free' medical service along with compulsory payment for the scheme that varies with the income of the citizen. But following Friedman, the focus of concern is not the provision of new packages *per se* but whether they are voluntary or involuntary; that is, whether or not there is free individual choice among existing goods and bads. The novelties offered by the welfare state may be designed to serve some laudatory purpose. But they cannot be regarded as voluntary packages; nor for that matter can the package consisting of the good (air-travel opportunity) along with the bads (noise) and other disamenities, such a package also being involuntary. It is entirely possible that a large number of people will, on balance, be made worse off by this involuntary package.

On reflection it becomes evident that, in respect of the B category of externalities, this general conclusion is independent of the method of solution proposed. As an instance, consider a favoured proposal of some economists, that of auctioning the property rights to a scarce resource. If, for example, the managers of industry (on behalf of the consumers of their products) outbid the inhabitants of a region for the property rights to the air shed above it, the allocation criterion appears to be met inasmuch as rights to the scarce resource, the region's clean air, are to be assigned to the party that places the higher value upon it.[22] Nevertheless, the inhabitants of the region, who will, of course, have the opportunity of buying the new products of the industry operating within the region, will also be compelled to suffer the resulting emissions of smoke and gases. They have no choice but to accept this package. And, again, there can be no presumption of an actual Pareto improvement.

Reference to examples of other externalities that are external to the activity, in particular the varieties of global risks — or, rather, the public's apprehension of such risks — currently associated with the products of recent technological progress, such as chemical pesticides, fluorocarbons, nuclear energy, add nothing but emphasis to this general conclusion. Placed on the market, the new products of man's ingenuity and enterprise may be said to extend the area of *market* choice. This is not all the same thing as offering free choice to individuals in respect of the packages of goods-*cum*-bads produced — much less the same as extending the area of individual choice.

Even if, as Friedman and others hope, the tide of government intervention is about to recede, and the private sector of the economy is about to expand at the expense of the government sector, there can be no assurance that, on balance, individual choice will grow. For in respect of externalities, associated with the products of new technology, there is also a concomitant contraction of non-market-goods choice. And it is at least arguable that, for a significant number of individuals, the loss of environmental choice outweighs, on the scale of welfare, the gain in market choice; that is, they would, if they had any choice in the matter, reject most of these new packages.

I conclude with a couple of observations. First, I have argued that the growth of external diseconomies, more particularly those external to the activity, shares with the growth of government the significant characteristic that it acts to reduce individual choice. But although each of these developments can be conceived of in isolation, they are in fact mutually reinforcing. The growth of government bureaucracy itself generates 'externalities' in the usually understood meaning of the term — externalities being the incidental effects on the welfare of individuals arising from the legitimate pursuit of economic activity. On the other hand, the growth of externalities, insofar as they create social hazards or conflicts of interest within the community, give rise to public demands for government regulation and control.

Second, in order to bring out the effct of externalities on individual choice in section VII, the assumption was made that (in the absence of government intervention) the relevant property rights are vested, initially, in the industry or, more generally, in the pollutor. This assumption is realistic enough bearing in mind the conventional presumption in favour of industrial expansion, the fact that much time may elapse before new externalities can be identified, the difficulties involved in tracing them to their source and the practical problems that arise in any endeavour to confer property rights on those who suffer the externalities associated with industrial growth and innovation.

This assignment of property rights, usually by default, to the industry or, more generally, to those whose activities directly cause the pollution, I have elsewhere referred to as L law — in contrast to an $\bar{L}$ law that would assign them, instead, to the victims of pollution.[23] With respect to allocation, the differences made to optimal solutions by adopting L̄ law rather than L law were then elaborated, assuming always that both welfare effects and transactions costs are entered into the calculus.

It remains only to bring out the point that if L̄ law prevailed in respect of all environmental externalities, individuals affected by such externalities would not suffer any effective diminution in their choice. For in virtue of the L̄ law, an individual would not have to suffer any adverse externality without his consenting to do so — a consent that the economist would take to be contingent upon his receiving adequate compensation, so maintaining his level of welfare. Such a law, could it be implemented, would then restore free individual choice amid growing environmental externalities.

However, even for a limited number of the more familiar environmental externalities, the effect of such legislation — assuming that it could be implemented — would be apt to curtail the production of certain goods quite drastically. Bearing in mind that transactions costs (including substantial information costs) would have to be borne now by the industry or pollutor, the resulting 'optimal' output of some goods might well be zero. Thus, the costs of extending individual choice by this legal device might, indeed, be heavy, even if industries could find ways of reducing pollution without necessarily reducing outputs.

On an allocation criterion, therefore a consideration of total conditions (or else the outcome of a collective decision) might well favour L law rather than L̄ law — notwithstanding which, those who, like Friedman, are deeply committed to individual freedom of choice might well favour L̄ law.

NOTES

1. Milton Friedman, *Free to Choose* (Harcourt Brace Jovanovich, 1979).

2. 'The Problem of Social Cost' (1960), 3, *J. Law & Econ.*, 1.

3. In a hypothetical economy of universal perfect competition, free of all externalities and government intervention, every exogenous change in the pattern of demand alone produces, in general, a corresponding set of product and factor prices that is also optimal or, more precisely, that meet the marginal conditions for optimality). Over time, then, the equilibrum and optimal prices of goods and factors rise and fall, as a result of which the choice-set facing individuals is altered, as is, also, the real distribution of income.

   Since little attention is paid by Chicago School economists to these possible changes in real income arising simply from ideal operation of the economic system, it may be reasonable to infer that they do not attribute much welfare significance to them, or else that any attempt to smooth out such price changes would be either unsuccessful or too costly relative to the benefits conferred. In the absence of exceptional economic circumstances, I would go along with this presumption. At all events, I would not regard such price changes over time as a valid criticism of Friedman's broad thesis. Indeed, they are implicitly excluded within a framework of partial economic equilibrium analysis that, following convention, is employed in this paper.

4. Garret Hardin, *The Limits of Altruism,* (Indiana University Press, 1977).

5. 'The Problem of Externality', *J. Law & Econ.*, 22 (1979), 141.

6. The word 'comprehensive' is used in this connexion to denote that all the relevant transactions costs are to be included in the calculation of net social benefit.

7. No economist need upset himself about this provisional semantic licence if he bears in mind that it enables me to identify and discuss the externality in the context of individual choice even where — according to the usuage mentioned above — such as externality has (allocatively speaking) been removed from the economy.

8. An apparently involuntary package may be effectively voluntary in that without government coercion each taxed person in the community would be willing to pay that tax as a price for the good provided by the government. An example would be that of a local government which provides a collective good, say a park, and levies on each family $10 a year in order to defray costs. If it is then sold to a private corporation on condition that the price of an annual ticket to use the park is set at $10, and the corporation discovers that each family in the community continues to buy a ticket, we infer that the initial involuntary package was effectively voluntary.

9. It is, of course, possible for the involuntary package to confer a *potential* Pareto improvement on society.

10. In the limiting case where the package reduces to a single item, the distinction between voluntary and involuntary, and their respective implications, continues to hold.

11. Some externalities happen to be both internal and external to the activity, but the extension of the analysis to cover this case is straightforward and need not detain us here. (The concepts of externalities internal and external to the activity, and their implications, were introduced in E.J. Mishan, 'Reflections of Recent Developments in the Concept of External Effects' *Can. J. Econ. & Pol. Sc.,* 31 (1965), 3.

12. The more flexible model for pollution problems, explicity regarded as being in the category of externalities that are external to the activity, is described and analysed in E.J. Mishan, 'What is an Optimal Level of Pollution' *J. Pol. Econ.,* 82 (1974), 1287.

13. This cost curve is, therefore, the marginal cost *excluding* rent which — as illustrated by H.J. Ellis and W. Fellner, 'External Economies and Diseconomies' *Am. Econ. Rev.,* 33 (1943), 493 — is equal to the average cost curve *including* rent.

14. For the purpose of formal comparison, I am ignoring the vital question of sustaining the yield of the fish population. I am assuming, therefore, that the increase in resources devoted to fishing, though it causes a decline in the average fishing catch, does not reduce the total fish population from year to year. This would be the case if it were possible to 'seed' the fishing grounds seasonally.

15. In Knight's model this price per journey is treated as a parameter and equal to the unchanged marginal valuation of the new highway to all motorists, given the conditions on the alternative routes. Monopoly revenue cannot therefore arise.

16. This smoke premium would, of course, have to be additional to the usual costs incurred by workers in moving their present location to the industrial centre in question.

17. In a general equilibrium model, the real wage is determined, *inter alia,* along with, and by reference to, all goods prices including the price of corn.

18. From a purely allocative standpoint, if the output of Smoke City in case (4') is optimal before smoke became a nuisance, it may also remain optimal afterwards. For the alternative of reducing output through workers moving from Smoke City (which is assumed here to be the only way of reducing the smoke damage they suffer) may be 'uneconomic' in the sense that the moving and

other costs incurred would exceed in value the benefits from moving.

19. *Supra,* n. 2.

20. It should be clear that if the farmer, and the man with the mountain view, each had claims to full compensation, their effective choice would not be reduced. We come across this point later in a more general context.

21. If the assumption of zero transactions-costs is removed, it is possible that the magnitude of such costs (for all conceivable ways of reducing noise) is so large that — on the relevant comprehensive allocative criterion — the optimal solution is, in fact, the existing unchecked noise damage.

22. Transferring the resource from the existing party to another who places a higher value upon it does not necessarily meet the conventional efficiency criterion of a potential Pareto improvement, since this requires that gainers from the transfer — assuming costless redistribution of gains — are able to compensate losers and yet remain better off. Thus, it may well be the case that an industry, on behalf of the consumers of its products, is able to offer as much as $2 billion for the rights to pollute an airshed over a region (up to some predetermined level), whereas the inhabitants of the region cannot offer more than $1.5 billion for the rights to use the airshed in order to protect themselves from the expected pollution. But since the effect on their welfare is critical, the minimum sum that they would need to restore their welfare to its original level if the pollution takes place could be well above the $2 billion that the industry could afford. If so, the efficiency criterion, properly understood as a potential Pareto improvement, is not met by the government's selling the rights to the airshed to the highest bidder. Put otherwise, if the rights to the airshed were already owned by the inhabitants, the industry could not afford to purchase them from the inhabitants.

   Once the assumption of zero transactions costs is removed, industry would be even less able to purchase the property rights from the region's inhabitants.

23. *See* E.J. Mishan, 'Optimality and the Law', *Oxford Econ. Papers,* 14 (1967), 255, and 'The Postwar Literature on Externalities: An Interpretative Essay', *J. Econ. Lit.,* 9 (1971), 1.

4 The Mystique of Economic Expertise

Regarded as a source of expertise, economics bristles with the earmarks of wordly success. As a means of global salvation, it commands more respect today than any ecumenical religion. Yet regarded as a science, as an empirical science at least, it has proved to be something of a fiasco. Certainly, any physical science which formulated so few dependable generalizations would be regarded by natural scientists with barely concealed amusement.

This seemingly cavalier judgment is sure to be resented by many who earn a living by teaching or practising the black art. The informed layman, the business executive or government official, in particular, is sure to think it intemperate. If, in an idle moment, he flicks through the pages of the prestigious economic journals, he is sure to be dazzled by the battalions of glittering symbols. Each year the proportion of words used in a theoretical economics papers seems to diminish. The huddled sentences that survive the expanding stairways of abstruse equations become fewer, and if any actual numbers appear, their intelligibility is soon dissipated in esoteric statistical tests. Certainly, the impression of precision and rigour conveyed by the professional economic literature is no less awesome than that which emerges from the pages of the journals of physics or biometrics.

Now, it is undeniable that over the last thirty years the formal sophistication of economic theory has made phenomenal strides. Refinements in general equilibrium theory encompassing hypothetical markets operating through time in all conceivable goods and bads, in options and in risk-bearing, continue to appeal to those seeking mathematical elegance. According to the mathematical form in which the models are cast, parametric limitations may be set of varying degrees of complexity within which 'local' and 'global' stability, and other desirable properties, are assured. Enterprising theorists will vie with one another in proposals to 'dynamise' such models or to divide them into an arbitrary though convenient number of broad sectors or, again, to study the conditions necessary to generate 'golden paths' along which the hypothetical economy will expand harmoniously at a constant rate for ever.

These ingenious constructs, descriptive of an economic never-never land, and rationalized as being in the nature of an analogue to an actual and imperfectly working market economy, admittedly provide no factual information or guidance for the public. At most, such models can claim heuristic value, and at least, the very least, an aesthetic appeal.

True, the popular technique of input-output analysis may be said to have been inspired by these general equilibrium models, but the usefulness of this oft-called 'tool of economic analysis', initially put together by Leontieff (a recent Nobel laureate) is itself debatable. The analysis purports to trace the required equilibrium size of each of the sectors into which an economy is divided, beginning with an exogenous set of final demands for the outputs of each sector. But how accurate and how reliable are the results?

Inevitably, perhaps, the economist's research and development took the form of increasing the complexity of the model: the number of sectors into which the economy is divided continued to increase, more detailed allowances being made for the government sector and the international-trade sector. The models were further elaborated to accommodate stocks as well as flows, to include pollutants, to bring in time more significantly, and so on.

Not surprisingly, however, the larger the number of

sectors and the greater the complexity generally, the less
dependable the forecasts. For the 'technical coefficients'
on which the results depend are those calculated over
some arbitrary period from the operation of the existing
economy. And, under conditions of rapid change, many
of the large number of technical coefficients can alter
significantly over a short span of time. Yet the limitations
of input-output models as instruments for forecasting the
detailed input requirements of the various sectors —
even with, or because of, continual revision of the coefficients — is not the only reason for scepticism. Although
government departments can hardly resist such models, if
only because their operation generates acres of numbers
requiring the services of teams of economists and
computer-operators, all of which help to promote
bureaucratic dominion, it is doubtful whether their findings have much impact either on the government's day-
to-day decisions or on its broad economic policy.

The same trend toward greater complexity is evident
also in the design of macroeconomic models to forecast
aggregate income, employment, investment and other
sectoral magnitudes that governments and businessmen
deem important. The performance of these high-powered
macroeconomic models are, of course, continually alleged
by their creators and proponents to be superior to the
'inspired guesses' of those adhering to more informal
methods. But the superiority is far from significant. What
is more pertinent, however, is that the critical parameters
of these models have to be updated every year or two by
reference to observed changes in the economy. Clearly,
the theory on which they are constructed is more theory
in form than in content. In effect, such a model is an
elaborate container that, while being fed with new
streams of data along with 'guestimates' about government and business plans, is itself under continual repair
and renovation. I do not decry the effort and the ingenuity of economists who erect and operate these models,
even though it is hard to believe that it would make much
difference to our economic progress if their forecasts
became more accurate or less. But it would be linguistically

licentious to bestow the status of scientist on the economist engaged in such forecasting techniques.

When it comes to the theory of price, or 'microeconomic theory' as it is called in the jargon, which addresses itself to the determination of the prices and the outputs of the variety of goods in competitive or non-competitive markets, the economist fares no better. Without firm theoretical foundations, he continues to foster the generalization that, *ceteris paribus,* the amount demanded of a good varies inversely with its price and the cognate proposition that an increase in the amount of an item acts to lower its relative value — a proposition that is, incidentally, basic to the familiar Quantity Theory of Money. Beginning with such basic propositions, the economist can elaborate models that yield quite complex forms of analysis relating the operation of factor and goods markets. But for all that, it does not enable the economist to foretell the changing pattern of outputs and relative prices.

The testing of even quite primitive hypotheses deducible from such stark axioms as individual consistency and insatiability poses difficulties which are overlooked by the standard economics textbook. This oversight is not altogether deliberate, since the author himself is more likely than not to be inured to the empirical anaemia of his subject and is not above passing off as significant test-statements uncovered by economic science such propositions as 'An attempt by the state to hold down market prices is apt to produce shortages and black markets' or 'A rise in the UK price level relative to that of the US acts to reduce the dollar value of the pound', along with other equally unremarkable insights.

We may throw in for good measure theorems raised upon the principle of comparative advantage which, with sufficient information, should enable the economist to predict the pattern of world trade, at least in the absence of trade barriers — even though it is hard to see what difference such prescience would make. In the event, such principles, and the factor-price theorems derived therefrom, serve only to 'explain', or rather to rationalize, what has happened or what is happening.

II

In sum, although economics employs the methods of the
sciences, although it has brought into being an impressive
amount of sophisticated theory, the implications of which
are at times subjected to exacting statistical tests, and
although there is a massive flow of information in the
form of magnitudes, indices, ratios, elasticities and the
like, this highly respectable academic discipline cannot
rightfully claim to produce dependable and significant
empirical laws. Such empiricism as has been captured
consists only of approximate relationships that with luck
survive a few short years from their estimation.

Thus, if economics is judged by the number of mono-
graphs or journal articles, by university enrolments or
media popularity, its future seems assured. Judged
instead by reference to its explanatory power and its
ability to control economic forces, its scientific record is
poor and its scientific prospects are bleak. The ambitious
economic research and the manifest bustle of university
and government departments may continue to attract the
attention and hope of an innocent public. But, surveying
this field of toil and endeavour, the detached and cynical
eye finds only profusion without order, energy without
direction, and innovation without progress. Indeed, a
romp through the professional journal literature today,
so resplendent in its technical regalia, invokes in the
mischievous mind the spectacle of a complex machine of
monstrous proportions assiduously engaged in renovating
itself, and while wantonly expanding in all directions,
advancing but little in any.

These half-derisive remarks, I hasten to add, are not
intended to cast aspersion on the integrity, the scholar-
ship and the ingenuity of the modern academic economist. The forlorn scientific prospects alluded to are the
unavoidable consequences of the nature of the subject
matter itself. Recognition of this depressing fact naturally
meets with psychological resistance. Indeed, one of the
abiding delusions of the young and eager economist is
that by pressing onwards, heedless of a disobliging

empiricism, he brings closer the day when economics will have earned its scientific spurs and the ungrudged respect of the scientific community.

In its methods, however, economics is, as already indicated, as mature as the natural sciences, but cannot come within bowling distance of their empirical range and accuracy; this is for the simple reason that whereas the physical universe is stable within the relevant time span, the 'economic universe', in contrast, is not. Indeed, the inconstancy of the measurable parameters of any economic system or model is aggravated by rapid technical change, by the vicissitudes of commercially inspired fashion, by switches in government policies and by political events at home and abroad. In the circumstances, the expertise offered by positive economics is restricted in its agenda, highly conditional, valid at best within wide margins of error and prone to increasing uncertainty. And if, notwithstanding, economists maintain a high profile in the world of affairs, their apparent self-assurance draws its animus less from scientific certitude and more from doctrinal conviction.

The increasing popularity and demand for economists by business and government cannot be explained, then, as a wholly rational phenomenon. Each age has its myths and its superstitions. If a spiritual age needs a priesthood to whom it can entrust its spiritual welfare, a secular age needs a priesthood to whom it can entrust its material welfare. What is more, the secular society we have inherited has become afflicted over the last few decades by quantomania, an affliction intensified by the so-called computer revolution. Figures impress people as never before, and most of all, they impress business executives and political bureaucrats. And, just because the economic world is in a continuous state of flux, economics is prodigious in the production and the revision of figures.

III

So far, we have been speaking of the expertise of the

economist in the way we would speak of the expertise of
the physicist, the biologist, the meteorologist or the
medical specialist. Such expertise takes the form of an
analysis of the expected consequences of introducing a
particular programme or policy under known conditions.
It is wholly in this sense that the Western democrat
voices the dictum about the expert being 'on tap but not
on top'. Strictly speaking, the expert provides the decision-
maker with information culled from the findings of scientific research. He does not recommend unless he is
required to do so by his terms of reference, and then
according to specified criteria.

The economist, however, apparently enjoys a status
distinct from that of other specialists in that he is
employed not only to pronounce on the consequences of
alternative policies — he is often expected also to rank
them on the scale of better or worse by reference to
economic criteria. Policy A, he might conclude, entails a
better allocation of the nation's resources than policy B,
or — which comes to the same thing — policy A is
economically more efficient than policy B. More impressive yet, the economist may extend himself so far as to
calculate the difference between two projects, A and B,
by attaching money magnitudes to them. He could, for
example, come up with the findings that the expected
stream of net benefits associated with A project has a
present value of £200 million, whereas that associated
with the B project has a present value of only £160
million. Since the projects cost the same, he will rank A
above B on the scale of better or worse.

The above paragraph describes the economist in his
evaluative capacity. In large part owing to the post-war
growth of environmental awareness in the Western
world, this branch of the discipline — familiar to the
profession as Welfare Economics — is in riotous blossom. Apart from contributions to its basic theoretical
analysis, there has been a burgeoning number of papers
and books on special aspects which apply and develop
this analysis. For instance, the subjects currently taught
as Public Finance, Urban Economics, Environmental

Economics, Transport Economics, Regional Economics, International Trade and Development Economics, build in large part on the concepts and constructs of Welfare Economics.

The formal problems to which the economist addresses his evaluating expertise fall into two broad categories: that concerned with ranking or evaluating one or more specific economic changes, and that concerned with determining some 'optimal' magnitude. The choices to be made within the former category are either those between alternative economic policies — whether, for example, to use an area of land for cash crops or for urban development, or whether to offer incentives to workers to move from rural areas to urban centres — or else those between alternative investment programmes; say, choosing between different types of dam systems all of which are technically feasible.

The second category of problems draws upon this same body of analysis so as to discover the necessary and sufficient conditions that identify an optimal solution. The particular problem may be that of determining an optimal inventory, an optimal fish population, an optimal yield of timber, an optimal flow of goods, an optimal level of pollution, an optimal location of an industrial plant or an airport, or an optimal time-path of consumption of some non-renewable resource such as coal or oil, to mention the more popular ones in the economic literature.

Although both categories of problem are usually analyzed within a partial economic context of varying degrees of restrictiveness; those in the former involve the application of allocative rules or cost-benefit methods, whereas those in the latter are generally cast in the form of maximizing (or minimizing) the value of some aggregate — the so-called 'objective function' — subject to technical, institutional and other constraints, an exercise that lends itself admirably to the calculus and related mathematical techniques.

Common to both kinds of problems, however, is the need for an economic evaluation of the social benefits conferred by the set of economic activities under inves-

tigation — the economic evaluation of social *costs,*
incidentally, being no other than the value of the social
benefits that are forgone when resources have to be
moved from their existing activities in order to contribute
to the new set of economic activities. Indeed, this notion
of an economic valuation of social benefits or costs is the
distinctive characteristic of that branch of the subject
which, as mentioned above, goes by the name of Welfare
Economics.

IV

If it is conceded that, when dispassionately assessed,
the claims of economics to be a positive science have to
be treated with sceptical reservation, it would be
reassuring both to the profession and to the public if, in
its evaluating capacity, the subject could reasonably be
assumed to shed light on important social problems
and, moreover, to have evolved practical techniques
for their solution.

Among the more urgent problems of the post-war
period are those related to the control of natural resources, the word 'resources' being used here to include
not only mineral deposits, soil, forests, everglades, fisheries, fresh water supplies and many species of flora and
fauna, but also other features of the biosphere in which
we are immersed and which is locally and globally polluted in varying degrees to the detriment of our health
and amenity.

Certainly, the environmental conscience of the public
has been aroused over this period, initially in the early
1960s by a small number of seminal works among which
are the books and articles written by ecologists such as
Rachel Carson, by biologists such as Garrett Hardin and
by one or two eccentric economists and engineers. Public
preoccupation has continued to grow, fed as it is by
frequent reports from all over the world of environmental disasters and expressed in a growing number of
newspaper and magazine articles, in popular books, in

official enquiries and in the establishment of environmental agencies and departments.

True, the world of big business may continue to endorse the views expressed by the irrepressible Milton Friedman, arch-representative of the Chicago School of economics, and other economists and thinkers of the Radical Right who, rightly alarmed at the encroaching power of the state, elect to believe that environmental concern today is misplaced and, indeed, that most of such problems can best be resolved by a strengthening of those two sovereign institutions, property rights and the competitive market. The business world also gives its blessing and its support to such incurable optimists as Julian Simons (whose argument that the growth of population and consumption, of itself, stimulates enterprise and innovation as to further enrich the world, at least materially, rests on little more than an unfastidious interpretation of economic indices and economic events over the past one hundred years or so) and technocrat Herman Kahn ever-impatient for the wonders and the challenge of the future. But on many environmental issues the business world seems today to be fighting a rearguard action against increasingly powerful environmental lobbies and the mounting concern of the public at large.

There is apparently no shortage of books just now on ecology, on the environment, and the alternative futures facing us. All too many of them, alas, are ill-informed and simplistic. Others are single-visioned, tracing the cause of our environmental woes to population growth or to the production of synthetics. Others, although providing vital information and excellent descriptions of ecological mechanisms, propose solutions that ignore political realities and take small account of the costs of their implementation.

Environmental concern, then, is not enough. By itself, it offers no assurance of environmental improvement. The seemingly irreconcilable claims of environmentalists, on the one hand, and business interests (including those of industrial workers) on the other, tend to issue in protracted conflict. In some instances this takes the form of militant confrontation, but more often, and especially in the USA, it takes the form of a massive legal battle in which a provisional victory to one of the contending parties acts only to inflame the other to greater efforts.

It is in virtue of the gathering intensity of such conflicts that the economist may prove to be a useful servant to society, an honest and informed broker, since by training he clearly perceives the opposition of interests to stem from economic activities that in the process of conferring commercial benefits on some, incidentally damage the amenity or interests of others. If the mountain of economic literature produced over the last two decades that addresses itself to the unwanted overspill of economic activity or, more generally, to the control of natural resources, can be taken seriously, this is the area in which the economist may yet vindicate his expertise and make a sterling contribution to society's welfare.[1]

V

The hub about which all this evaluating expertise turns, however, is the concept of economic efficiency. If one project is ranked above another by reference to a standard definition of 'economic efficiency', it may well be argued that the term *'economic efficiency'* is purely descriptive. Yet it is hard to ignore the commendatory connotation that follows from the consideration that more efficiency is, presumably, preferred to less.

The innocent layman might reasonably suppose that on so fundamental a concept as the criterion of economic efficiency there would be either basic agreement within the profession or else raging controversy, for unless such criterion can claim legitimacy the conclusions reached by economists in this vital area of resource allocation cannot be taken seriously. In fact there is neither — only some desultory sniping from time to time. Among the many writers today who have recourse to a criterion for ranking alternative organizations, few give much thought to this question of legitimacy. Schools of engineering, of business, of sociology, of psychology, of planning and of systems analysis all contribute their quotas of enthusiastic writers who direct their ingenuity to solving problems that may properly be subsumed under Welfare Economics. For the most part such writers appear to accumulate a variety of techniques over time, like parts of a Meccano set, until they are inspired to construct some *ad hoc* working model for a particular purpose. Even among economists writing within the area of resource allocation — the more practical part of Welfare Economics — there is far more emphasis on analytic sophistication than on the crucial rationale and justification of the criterion employed or proposed.

Now, the economic criterion that is far and away the most popular is the *net benefit* criterion. It is the one actually employed by economists in evaluating and ranking alternative projects or programmes, and it is, incidentally, disarmingly simple. By skirting the implications of a familiar valuation paradox — such implications if anything strengthening a sceptical conclusion — the simplicity and appeal of this criterion may be illustrated by an example of an economic change affecting a community consisting, say, of only three persons. To person A, we suppose, the change is welcome and worth £50 (this sum being the most he is willing to pay for the change). Person B also gains by this change to the tune of £30. On the other hand, person C loses £60 by the change in question (this sum being the minimum necessary to reconcile him to it). The algebraic aggregate of these three sums — £50 plus £30 minus £60 — is equal to *plus* £20. This £20 is then the *positive* net benefit to the community arising from this economic change.

It goes without saying that the 'optimal' solution, or most efficient solution, to a problem encompassing a number of alternative aggregate valuations of this sort can be determined by the same net benefit criterion. For, by definition, this optimal solution is one that yields the *highest* net benefit attainable under the conditions specified.

For the evaluating economist, then, the relevant 'objective' data are nothing more than the subjective valuations of the persons affected by the change, his particular skill and ingenuity being addressed to more accurate ways of calculating them.

The reader will have noticed, however, that the net-benefit figure as illustrated above is calculated without reference to any distributional consequences. For example, it makes no difference to the resulting sum of £20 whether person C who loses £60 by the change is very much poorer than persons A and B who gain by it. We could therefore proceed quite properly to appraise the net benefit criterion in disregard of its associated distributional effects, as indeed is the practice in current applications to problems of resource allocation and project evaluation. Yet this aspect is worth touching upon since it continues to provoke argument and to generate formal analyses and proposals by economists and philosophers.

Thus, among the ways proposed to modify the net-benefit criterion so as to make provision for the distributional effects, two continue to be popular among those economists concerned with its application to the ranking of investment projects. The first, which is associated with Little's famous *Critique of Welfare Economics* (1950), is the proposal that in addition to the net-benefit criterion an independent distributional criterion be met — a dual criterion in effect. The second proposal, which can trace its lineage to the eminent Cambridge economist, Alfred Marshall, is that of converting money values into 'real' values by multiplying the money valuation of each person's gain or loss by a weight that is to be set by reference to that person's income. In our example, if person C were much poorer than A or B, the real satisfaction he derives from an additional pound of income is assumed to be higher than that for an additional pound accruing to persons A or B. As the old-time economist would put it, person C's 'marginal utility' of money is higher than that of A or B. The effect of this proposal, then, is to convert the original net-benefit criterion in money units into a utility-weighted net benefit criterion which, since the units of measure are in terms of utility (or 'real' satisfaction), we may call a 'net-utility criterion.'

Clearly, the application of each of these two distinct criteria — the standard net-benefit criterion and the net utility criterion — to a particular economic change can produce contrary results. Returning to our simple example again, if we assessed the utility of each pound of the £60 loss to person C from the change as equal to three times the utility of each of the additional pounds gained either by A or by B from the change, the aggregate in utility terms (equating a pound to A or B to one 'util') becomes the algebraic summation of 50 for A *plus* 30 for B *minus* 180 for C, a net utility of *minus* 100. In contrast, therefore, to the net-benefit criterion of *plus* £20, which pronounces this particular change to be economically efficient, this net-utility criterion values the change at a loss of 100 utils and consequently pronounces the change to be economically *in*efficient.

Now, since, as it turns out, our conclusions remain the same whether the net-benefit criterion continues to be used or whether, instead, any of the proposed net-utility criteria comes to be adopted, and since in any case the propositions and the techniques to be found in the economic literature are expounded for the greater part in money terms, we shall continue to direct our criticisms, in the main, towards the standard net-benefit criterion. Later on, however, we shall find it instructive to digress briefly in order to disclose the implications of recent proposals to introduce a set of weights into economic evaluation by reference to political objectives.

VI

The first thing to realize in this sort of investigation is that the rationale of the net benefit criterion, about which the question of legitimacy turns, appears to differ according to whether we regard the theory of resource allocation, or more generally Welfare Economics itself, to be a part of positive economics or to be, instead, a normative branch of economics.

The earlier conception of Welfare Economics, that developed by Marshall (1890) and adhered to by later Cambridge economists, chiefly Pigou and Robertson, seemed to place it within the boundary of positive economics. Certainly, the ostensible purpose of their analyses was to deduce propositions that would serve to guide economic policy, and in this way to make a contribution to society's welfare. Although the original development of the subject was embedded in a utility foundation, Sir John Hicks in 1939 convincingly argued that the analytic structure would stand more firmly on alternative foundations; in effect, on the net-benefit criterion itself, unemcumbered by the older Cambridge propositions that necessarily involved assumptions about 'interpersonal comparisons of utility' — that is, about attributing a utility index or a utility ranking to a sum of money gained or lost according to the individual's income. For such utility comparisons were unacceptable to many economists of a later generation and were, in any case, impossible to verify. The relatively unchanged structure of the theory when raised on these new foundations was subsequently referred to as the 'New Welfare Economics'.

Let us now turn to the basic hypothesis which is common to both the Old and the New Welfare Economics. Inasmuch as a positive net benefit continues to be interpreted as an increase in *real* income for the community, this hypothesis can be read as stating that an increase in real income, other things being equal, increases social welfare. Although stated casually so that it may escape challenge, such a hypothesis is in fact highly dubious. Certainly, it cannot be subject to an empirical test, there being no acceptable measure of social welfare that is also definitionally distinct from real income or net benefit. Nevertheless, the ambitious welfare economist sought both to cover his flanks from attack and to promote the plausibility of this hypothesis by making it contingent upon a number of conditions, conditions that he might suppose would be met or roughly met in the relevant circumstances.

One condition is that 'economic man' — a shorthand

for the individual acting in his economic capacity — is the best judge of his own economic interests and that therefore his own valuations alone ought to count in respect of any economic change. Insofar as the change in question is restricted to the prices of meat, tomatoes, tobacco or beer, this condition is likely to be met. But bearing in mind that many of us spend a good part of our lives unwishing decisions we have made in the past, the confidence that can be reposed in the judgment of our economic man increasingly declines the more significant is the effect of his decisions on his style of life and his moral development.

A second condition is that over the relevant period of time economic man's tastes do not alter. It is possible that the effect on a man's welfare of say a public project, initially conceived by him as a stream of benefits, may later be revalued by him, in consequence of a change in his tastes, as a stream of losses. This contingency is far from being unlikely. Even in a relatively static or tradition-bound society, the cycle of life itself produces changes of taste and feeling so that, unless a person is guided by the experience and wisdom of others, disappointments can arise from his making provision for things that would soon fail to gratify. As Johnson bluntly put it, 'The young man does not care for the child's rattle, and the old man does not care for the young man's whore.'

This problem can be fudged by supposing that over time both the age structure and the income structure of the community do not vary much so that the resulting 'taste profile' remains much the same — at least with respect to the products and by-products of the economic projects being contemplated. But although this device may be plausible enough for a tradition-bound society, it is far from being acceptable for a commercial and rapidly innovating society, one in which for given age-groups there are continual changes in tastes and values.

A third and last condition is that, in assessing the net benefit of a proposed project, each and every effect on people's welfare has to be counted. This is a tall order. Clearly, the larger the scope and the duration of a

project, the harder it is for the economist to estimate the
stream of individual valuations over time. In the economic evaluation, for instance, of a major new airport it
is feasible — even allowing for some uncertainty about
future behaviour and developments — to make estimates
of the worth of better travel facilities and also of the
more familiar disamenities such as an increase of noise or
the resiting of homes. There are, however, the less
tangible aesthetic, ecological and sentimental considerations that undoubtedly affect people's welfare but which
economists have difficulty in quantifying. Although the
forward-looking technocrat may dub such attitudes as
'irrational', the economist cannot properly exclude them.
Indeed, if he were able to put reasonable figures on these
intangibles, they might well be such as to outweigh the
net figure for the more measurable items.

VII

The above reflections open the mind to the possibility of
founding Welfare Economics explicitly upon value judgments. But whose value judgments? Those of the writer,
those of the planner or bureaucrat, those of the professional economist or those of the community itself?

It is, of course, entirely possible for a writer to propose
a criterion that is of interest to himself if only because he
believes he has the research facilities for discovering if a
particular number of alternative proposals meets his
chosen criterion. This notion of a criterion, however, is
acceptable only if we are interested primarily in providing employment opportunities for economists. It is
hardly necessary to remark that a personal and therefore
an arbitrary criterion cannot be taken seriously if,
instead, we are interested in the welfare of society as a
whole. This being the case, a criterion formulated by a
bureaucrat or by any professional body, especially one
designed to give expression to their own particular value
judgments, would also be regarded as something of an
impertinence, at least in a Western democracy. Thinking

along such lines we should have to conclude that the search for a welfare criterion based on acceptable value judgments has ultimately to be referred to the prime source of authority, the community itself acting either as a body politic or else in some other capacity.

Acting in a political capacity the community may well sanction the existing standard economic criterion; indeed, it would appear overtly to do so whenever it commissions the economist to undertake a cost-benefit study of a project or programme. To be sure, the political decision-makers are not constitutionally bound to follow the economist's conclusions. They are free to reject his ranking of alternative projects and his cost-benefit findings, and they frequently do so. Nonetheless, this sort of economic expertise tends to be regarded by the public as a non-political contribution to the decision-making process.

Accepting such a belief, it would follow that if the political process rejects the findings of the economist, the latter may rightly claim (assuming, always, that his calculations are correct) that, whatever other advantages are claimed for it, the government's decision is one that is *economically* inefficient — since projects or policies that fail to meet the economist's criterion are, by definition, inefficient.

What influence is exerted by the economist's criterion would appear to depend, therefore, upon the extent of its acceptability by society in some *non*-political capacity. Incontrovertible acceptability is assured only if this criterion follows from value judgments to which the community as a whole subscribes — value judgments, therefore, that transcend changes in political alignment and opinion. One is impelled to conclude, then, that nothing less than an ethical consensus is needed to confer legitimacy on the economist's criterion. For only such a consensus enables him to assert with authority that, irrespective of the political support they currently attract, particular projects or policies are economically inefficient.

VIII

It is instructive at this juncture to turn aside for a moment in order to appraise recent proposals to use politically determined weights in transforming the standard net-benefit criterion into what we have called a 'net utility criterion', since the employment of such weights acts to blur the distinction we are trying to draw as between economic efficiency and political desirability. It transpires that where such weights are directly or indirectly politically determined the economics is, in effect, swallowed up whole by the politics — although this may not always be obvious to the public or even to the economist.

True, it may seem on first thoughts prudent, to say the least, to use distributional and other weights in the endeavour to balance the benefits to some individuals against the losses to others. And again, it may be thought reasonable that such weights be calculated by reference to the priorities evinced by political decision-makers themselves, as has been proposed by a number of competent economists[2], usually on the argument that the weights to be chosen should be guided by the objectives of 'the national plan'.

It is a revealing comment on the myopia that comes with absorption in the technicalities of analysis that the repeated attempts by some economists to extend the authority of their cost-benefit calculations by recourse to such political weights would, if successful, render them all but impotent as economists. For they would then perforce have to confine their expertise to disclosing inconsistencies, if any, in the initial set of weights derived from or proposed by the political decision-makers. But once this is done, there is no longer an independent economic criterion by which the resulting (consistent) set of investment plans can be assessed.

Moreover, some duplicity is perpetrated, albeit unwittingly. Admittedly, the requirement of consistency in the selection of weights imposes some discipline on policy-makers and may therefore lead to some revision of their investment plans. But this consistency desideratum should, if anything, act to reinforce political bias. Where basic policy is misconceived, a search for consistency acts only to extend the damage. We should bear in mind, besides, that not only distributional weights have been proposed but also 'merit', ethnic and other weights. With the post-war trend towards more populist politics, we cannot discount the possibility of future agitation in favour of 'gay' weights, feminist weights, single-parent weights, and so on. For that matter, neither would the cunning bureaucrat or politician be above trying to smuggle in a pet project or two by proposing a brand new weight on the pretext of some exceptional characteristic.

Taken at their face value, the consequences of such proposals are as paradoxical as they are ironic. They would enable politicians in office to shape the resulting economic criterion to their hearts' desire. Indeed, rather than an independent economic criterion being used to select investment projects from a set proposed by politicians, the politically proposed set of projects itself is now used to select an economic criterion — one that (subject to the consistency constraint) necessarily ensures their 'economic' acceptability.[3]

Economic expertise cooked to a recipe that imparts quantitative rationalization to the economic policies favoured by the political incumbents may well serve to enhance the popularity of economists among the political establishment. But it would do so at the cost of his professional integrity and, eventually, of his credibility.

IX

We have to remind ourselves, however, that political independence of the economic criterion is only one of the desirable features it must possess; general acceptability is another. In this connexion, it is worth recording that it was once believed that if a proposed change met the economist's net-benefit criterion and if, in addition, the resulting distribution of income was at least no worse,

then it could be inferred that the change would also make
everyone actually better off.[4] Since an economic change
that would actually make everyone better off without
making the resulting distribution of income any worse
would have a strong if not a universal appeal, the economist's net-benefit criterion (at least when supplemented by the distributional proviso) would seem to rest
on secure foundations. Alas for those short-lived heady
days! The reasoning turned out to be flawed, and the net-
benefit criterion went wandering off in search of more
solid foundations.

   To cut the story short, it has since been suggested that
the net-benefit criterion itself might be said to embody an
acceptable value judgment inasmuch as an economic
change that yields a positive net benefit is also one that
— if transfer payments were costless — could be so
redistributed as to make everyone actually better off.[5]
Thus, if this corollary of a positive net benefit were
generally believed to be a good thing for society, the net-
benefit criterion itself could be said to command a consensus. If the criterion did command a consensus, the
hand of the economist would indeed be strengthened.
The resulting mandate to employ the net-benefit criterion,
moreover, dispenses with any need of those dubious
assumptions of fact required to support the so-called
objective conception of Welfare Economics. We can
immediately jettison, that is, the basic hypothesis of this
objective conception that an increase in real income (or
net benefit) contributes to society's welfare in the
ordinary sense. Nor do we need to suppose either (1) that
each man is the best judge of his own welfare or (2) that
over the relevant time period his tastes remain unaltered.
Suffice it that the net-benefit criterion itself commands a
consensus.

   The implications of this so-called normative approach
can bear emphasis. The economist himself is not to be
thought of as prescribing for the good of society in the
way a physician, say, prescribes for the health of his
patient. On the contrary, the economist would want to
guard himself against any charge of arrogance in presuming

to prescribe or to recommend particular economic arrangements for the benefit of society. Rather, we should imagine his addressing the community after this fashion: 'According to the criterion that you, the community, have agreed upon, namely the net-benefit criterion, investment project A is ranked above project B, and project B above project C...' Thus, although the economist concludes his report by ranking the projects in the order, A, B, C., this form of conclusion is to be understood as an abridgment of the quoted sentence.

In the light of the above remarks, the difference between the so-called objective conception and the so-called normative conception of the subject begins to narrow. In both conceptions, after all, economists are directing their analysis to discover the sorts of economic change that meet a social goal believed to command a consensus. But whereas in the objective case the social goal is explicitly the unexceptionable if inoperative one of increasing 'social welfare', in the ordinary sense, in the normative case the social goal becomes the more operative concept of an increase in aggregate net benefit. Nonetheless, some dissimulation — we need remind ourselves — is involved in the former (the objective) case. Not only do conditions (1) and (2) above have to hold over the relevant period, the calculated net benefit is assumed *as a judgment of fact* to raise society's well-being, an assumption that is, incidentally, made the more specious by substituting for positive net benefit such synonyms as 'an increase in real income' or 'an increase in economic efficiency'. In the latter (normative) case, in contrast, since there are no questionable assumptions or conditions, there can be no dissimulation. That which is held to elicit a consensus is no more than the net-benefit criterion itself.

It must be recognized, however, that there are other components of a consensus that may occasionally conflict with an economic change that would meet the net-benefit criterion. An economic arrangement by which a group of men are willing to sell themselves into slavery to others could be one that meets the net-benefit criterion, but it is also one that would affront the conscience of the community. It would therefore have to be rejected by the economist who expressly draws his sanction from the ethical code of the community. (Alternatively, it may be argued that such an arrangement would in fact fail to meet the net-benefit criterion simply because the abhorrence of all others who are not included in this private transaction has properly to be entered into the calculation).

X

To the crucial question whether or not the net-benefit criterion, which is continually used by economists, does in fact command a consensus, or could be made to do so, there is as yet no convincing answer. Were a survey to be taken, it may well be rejected as being unsatisfactory on grounds of equity since it is not impossible that for some of the economic changes that would be countenanced by the criterion-significant losses would be suffered by the poor. On the other hand, if the question were thoroughly debated before the survey, it might be concluded that — as a judgment of fact — continued application of the criterion within the existing institutional framework offers the best hope for raising living standards and not least among the economically underprivileged.

Be that as it may be, we cannot dismiss the possibility that a consensus would not be forthcoming. Within a modern economy there are some who believe, not without reason, that norms of taste and propriety are declining and that much of the nation's output is trivial if not regrettable. There can therefore be dissent to the basic requirement of the criterion that the valuation of every member of the community has to be entered into the calculation. If, for example, the net-benefit criterion happened to favour an expansion of investment in pornographic cinema, in abortion facilities, in repatriating ethnic groups or in homosexual pleasuredromes, there might be large numbers of citizens who would reject the validity of the criterion.[6]

Recent changes in social attitudes tend to reinforce the suspicion that the consensus necessary to vindicate the economist's criterion, assuming it ever existed, is dissolving. First, there is greater reluctance today among segments of the public — made explicit in debates between economists, lawyers and political scientists — to accept without strong reservations the judgment of the market (in which the demand for a good is the sum of individual valuations) when account is taken of substantial expenditures on commercial advertizing. Second, there is the topical question of the current depletion rates of a variety of natural resources. Prior to the Second World War, the question was generally regarded as being of academic interest. But the present scale of industrial consumption of natural resources has made it a subject of deep concern to the public at the same time as it has become one of controversy within the ranks of economists.[7]

This division of opinion among those within the economics profession turns on the question of whether the conventional procedure of discounting anticipated future benefits and losses continues to be valid when different generations are affected by the project under consideration. It can be argued that on grounds both of equity and of allocation the conventional economic rationale for using discount rates collapses.[8]

Third, there is a growing realization that inasmuch as the untoward consequences of consumer and producer innovations tend to unfold slowly over time — this being notoriously true for food additives, for chemical drugs, pesticides, synthetic materials and (if we include the intangible yet potent effects) for a variety of new gadgets — their valuation at any point of time by the buying public or the ordinary citizen may bear little relation to the benefits actually enjoyed over time. In general, it may be said that the very pace of innovation makes it all but impossible for the buying public to learn from its experience, and therefore to assess the relative merits of a large proportion of the goods coming onto the market. In consequence, a belief that continued application of the net-benefit criterion — or, for that matter, the continued operation of competitive markets — will act over time to raise society's well-being is more a statement of faith than of dispassionate judgment.

XI

Now, if it is indeed the case that the required consensus can no longer be mustered, if ever it could, and that therefore the net-benefit criterion can not be vindicated by reference to a wide ethical appeal, the authority of the evaulating economist is diminished. He must abandon any claim to being able to employ an economic criterion that transcends political opinion, from which it follows that there can no longer be legitimate economic norms of resource allocation independent of those proposed by political decision-makers.

In the event, the subject of Welfare Economics has to assume a humbler role, one that is consonant with economics conceived as being wholly a positive discipline. It has to shed any pretence to being a prescriptive study and must reconcile itself to being a wholly neutral study, its familiar propositions, including the economic criterion itself, being regarded as no more than *descriptive*. Such propositions are then pertinent only if political decision-makers assert that they are.

To be plain about it, if an economic change is correctly calculated to yield a positive net benefit, the economist is of course quite at liberty to say as much. What he may no longer do, however, is to argue as if the net-benefit criterion were a legitimate norm of policy for the community, or even a desirable feature of an economic change. For example, apart from directing his expertise to estimating the distributional effects of a particular policy, our neutral economist may well allege that it does not produce a positive net benefit or that alternative policies would produce larger net benefits. Such allegations, whether correct or not, are after all unambiguously positive statements. They will be relevant to economic policy, however, only insofar as one of the current goals of government is to produce larger net benefits, and they will be relevant to society at large only insofar as society itself is currently concerned about net benefits.

The economist may indeed continue, perversely perhaps, to use the term 'economic efficiency' in his professional writings. Yet in a neutral Welfare Economics, the term is no more than a shorthand for the algebraic sum of individual valuations when positive. Certainly, the term ought then to be restricted to the professional literature since for the general public it is bound to carry normative overtones.

XII

A conclusion that economic expertise — conceived as deriving from a legitimate body of economic theory specifically developed to offer independent means of evaluating and ranking alternative economic arrangements, and therefore also of determining optimal solutions — is at best a fragile thing is a conclusion that errs on the side of restraint. True, there is some intellectual satisfaction to be had from thinking through the conditions under which the standard economic criterion would in fact become a robust and serviceable instrument in raising society's welfare. Such an exercise, however, would serve to confirm the belief that these conditions are not to be found in the world we inhabit.

Yet even if it were possible somehow to banish all doubt about the validity and the comprehensiveness of the economist's criterion, a realization of the restrictive framework within which it operates should temper our optimism. For one thing, the economist's familiar optimality techniques are developed within a model that treats both population and its consumption, or their rates of growth over time, as *exogenous* factors. This means that although their existing magnitudes or their future growth rates, as estimated by the economist, are essential parts of his model, they are not among the things that are to be controlled in the optimal solution.

A philosophic mind would be drawn to this interesting fact that in all such optimising models, and therefore also in those designed to reveal the optimal time-path of resource consumption, the only acceptable constraints are technological, ecological and institutional. Certainly, no constraint on appetite need be considered for a moment. In the high-technology countries of the West, at least, the agenda of the economist in times of peace does not include the devising of limits on consumption in general. Quite the contrary, the sort of economic future to which governments both in 'developed' and 'lesser developed' countries are committed is invariably one that envisages a secular growth of consumption.

Over the last two centuries, however, the economic growth experienced by the West may be said to have succeeded only too well in creating a civilization characterized by mass affluence, since it is also becoming increasingly frantic, tasteless, unruly and extravagant. Any sober proposals today to create for ourselves a more sensible way of life — one designed among other things to unclutter the streets and skies, to curb the clamour, to reduce the traffic fume and to ease the tension — would require that we jettison much of our covetted hardware, our engines and our labour-saving machinery. Such proposals are, of course, at variance with the ethos of a science-based civilization which extols 'motivation' and innovation. They would be attacked by all political parties as being 'elitist', as being a covert assault — especially at a time of 'widespread hardship' — on the living standards of the mass of ordinary people struggling for the 'good things of life'.

Yet the fact remains — to take but one instance — that the danger of a global energy crisis arises, in the last resort, just because we are unable to call a halt to our material aspirations, just because we have come to adopt a style of living that is predicated upon the prodigal consumption of energy and materials, consumption that will be accelerated by the current diffusion of computer technology.

It is of ancillary interest to note in this connexion that

this growing demand for energy is being augmented in the USA by the recent rise of population there, by far the greater part of the increase being the result of illegal immigration (estimated to be over 2 million in the year 1982-83 alone, mainly Hispanics). In the event, it should not prove hard to rationalize by standard economic arguments the proposed industrial and mining incursion into some thousands of square miles of once-reserved territories in Nevada, Utah, Colorado and elsewhere.

Thus the expertise of the evaluating economist, even assuming it could be vindicated, offers no reassurance whatever to those who are genuinely concerned with the preservation of those attributes — variety, amenity, security, access to areas of natural beauty — that are basic to wholesome living. For in a world where controls on population and consumption are not to be seriously contemplated, the economist's ideal solution is consistent with a future of increasing rates of resource depletion and of increasing pollution and disamenity. In such a world, then, effective application of the economist's optimality techniques — assuming, again, they are valid — may properly be described as a means of making the best of a continuously worsening situation.

NOTES

1. Partha Dasgupta's recent book, *The Control of Resources* (Blackwell, 1982), is worth glancing through in this connexion, its being in many ways representative of the current body of professional literature in this field and admirably representing its virtues and defects.

2. In particular, by the authors of the UNIDO Manual, *Guidelines for Economic Evaluation* (New York, 1971).

3. Moreover, since the mechanism of the market acts so as to operate the standard net-benefit criterion (allowances being made for differences in the degree of monopoly, excise tax and externalities), acceptance of such a proposal would subject the

economy as a whole to two different economic criteria. The
suggestion that while the net-benefit criterion continues to apply
in the private sector of the economy, the public sector should be
guided, instead, by this net-utility criterion may be dismissed as
sophistry, at least when it is recognized that a major economic
problem is that of allocating resources between the public and
private sector. Although other considerations will indeed enter
into so important a decision, the economist cannot resolve this
allocation problem without a prior agreement as to which of the
two (potentially contradictory) criteria is to be employed.

4. Those interested in the recent history of this development should
    begin with I.M.D. Little's Critique of Welfare Economics (Oxford
    University Press, 1957). Expositional considerations have
    prompted me to be less fastidious in presenting the summary
    version above than I would be in a professional economic journal.
    Yet the text is not misleading. Those who have not followed the
    debate that ensued, in particular its course between the years
    1950 and 1965, might find it useful to begin with my 1965 article in
    Oxford Economic Papers, 'The Recent Debate on Welfare
    Criteria'.

5. Or as Kaldor, who proposed this test of 'hypothetical compen-
    sation' (in the *Economic Journal* of 1939) put it, the gainers from
    the change could compensate the losers and still remain better off
    than they were before the change.
       In this connexion it is of some interest to remark that even
    among competent economists the belief continues that the net-
    benefit criterion is one that implicity assumes a *uniform* weighting
    of gains and losses irrespective of a person's income. (For a recent
    example, *see* Dasgupta's *Control of Resources.)* The main purpose
    of Kaldor's famous note, however, was to show that this interpre-
    tation of uniform weighting — as explicitly advanced by Harrod in
    the same journal in 1938 — was unnecessary, and to propose an
    alternative 'hypothetical compensation' interpretation as the
    effective rationale of the criterion.

6. The first impulse of an academic economist in response to the
    above paragraph (main text) is to seek to maintain the credibility
    of the net-benefit criterion simply by classifying such forms of
    outrage and dissent as no more than a type of 'negative extern-
    ality'. This is not the case, however. Any negative externalities
    that arise in these examples express only the loss (measured as a
    compensatory sum of money) suffered by these citizens in con-
    sequence of introducing projects that they deplore — such extern-
    alities admittedly being consistent with an agreement by all
    members of society to count everybody's valuation.

If now, however, there are groups within society that no longer respect the values placed on the various goods or bads by other groups and, therefore, do not agree that the valuations of members of these other groups should enter the calculus at all, it is the validity of the net-benefit criterion itself that is being challenged.

7. An example about the controversies about advertizing, and especially about whether it should be regarded as an aspect of free speech, is the short volume, *Advertizing and Free Speech* ed. A, Hyman and M. Bruce Johnson (Lexington Books, 1977). For a review and bibliography of the 'anti-establishment' literature on resource depletion, the reader cannot do better than to consult Talbot Page's *Conservation and Economic Efficiency* (Resources for the Future, 1977).

8. For example, even the simplest imaginable case in which over successive generations there is a uniform rate of time-preference (exactly equal to an unchanging rate of return on investment), the discounted present value of future benefits can no longer be interpreted as a hypothetical gain or loss — a hypothetical gain being one that could make everyone better off (assuming costless transfers). A net gain has, in these circumstances, to be interpreted instead as a *hypothetical* hypothetical improvement since it requires hypothetical *intra*-generational transfers and hypothetical *inter*-generational transfers in order to actualize its potential.

Clearly, the interpretation of this sort of discounted net-benefit figure has less appeal even than the standard (undiscounted) net-benefit figure. As such, the economist's criterion, in its discounted form, is not likely to command a consensus among all populations affected through time.

A simple exposition of this argument can be found in my *Introduction to Normative Economics* (Oxford University Press, 1981), Part IX.

5   G N P: Measurement or Mirage?

What, since the middle of this century, has become the prime measure of a nation's overall excellence? There can be only one answer: its GNP. What today is the goal towards which all governments strive with indefatigable purpose? Again, there can be only one answer: the goal of increasing the growth of its GNP.

In all the industrial nations, battalions of economists are wholly occupied in forecasting GNP, in analyzing in tortuous detail the economic implications of the annual, quarterly and monthly changes in its components. But just what is this GNP stuff which exerts so hypnotic an effect on our diurnal aspirations? Just what is it supposed to measure? And just what significance can be attributed to those year-to-year changes in GNP?

CONVENTIONAL INTERPRETATION AND CONVENTIONAL ADJUSTMENTS

When expressed in 'real' terms — that is, when calculated at factor prices (or prices net of goods taxes) and 'deflated' by an index of factor prices — the figure for GNP has long been regarded by the business world as an overall index of the nation's economic performance during the year. The intelligent citizen who casually follows the reported movements in GNP cannot, however, be assumed entirely innocent. He does not expect the coverage to be complete and the calculation exact. He is not much surprised when told by experts that estimated GNP could be in error by as much as 10 per cent or more either way of the 'true' GNP figure. For

108

example, an overpricing of services provided by the public sector acts to overstate the official GNP figure, whereas transactions taking place in the so-called black economy (where services are exchanged for cash in order to evade taxes) clearly act to understate GNP.

But these concessions to possible inaccuracies in the computation tend rather to incline the citizen to think of the GNP figure as an imperfect estimate of what is, in the last resort, a clearly definable magnitude — a hard figure indicative of the full extent of the nation's economic activity. If this in fact is a delusion, he can hardly be blamed for it. After all, the *nominal* figure for GNP — prior, that is, to correction by a price index — is indeed defined as the aggregate expenditure (gross) on finished goods during the year. And this gross expenditure is known to bear a close relation to the aggregate of personal incomes over the same period.

Actually, the more relevant measure of aggregate economic activity is not GNP but NNP, or net national product, the latter being equal by definitional accounting to net national income or the sum of all personal incomes; for GNP itself is the aggregate expenditure over the year both on consumer goods and on *gross* investment (which includes additions to inventories) as a result of which some double-counting is necessarily involved. This is because the nominal value of the finished consumer goods produced during the year includes sums that are attributed to capital amortization, and this amortization figure is *roughly* equal to the annual expenditure on 'replacement capital'. But this 'replacement capital' figure appears again in *gross* investment along with new additions to capital. Thus, by adding to the total expenditure on consumer goods the figure for gross investment instead of the figure for *net* investment (net additions to the capital stock) we are counting 'replacement capital' roughly twice — including it as the amortization component in the value of consumer goods and again as the replacement-capital component, along with new capital goods, in gross investment.[1] We may conclude, therefore, that GNP exceeds the more relevant measure of eco-

nomic performance, NNP, roughly by the figure for
annual amortization costs — notwithstanding which,
since economists are mainly interested in *changes* over
time or in country-wise comparisons, we may follow
convention and accept *differences* in GNP to be a good
proxy for differences in NNP.

Among the standard adjustments is that of reducing
the nominal value of a country's GNP to 'real' GNP for
the purpose, say, of comparing it with the real GNP of an
earlier year. As indicated earlier, this requires that we
divide the nominal GNP by an index of the price changes
that have taken place between the two periods being
compared. Since in general all prices do not change in the
same proportion, the calculated price index will vary
according to the relative weight attributed to the price-
change of each of the goods in the index. By using as a
basis for computing GNP weights that are proportional to
expenditures on each class of goods in the first year, and
then weights that are proportional to such expenditure in
the second year, it is possible to obtain quite different
figures for the *change* in GNP as between the two years.
Indeed, it is possible that the adoption of 'base date'
weights (calculated, say, from relative expenditures in
1972) produces a GNP figure for 1972 that is below that
for 1973, whereas the adoption instead of 'reference date'
weights (calculated from relative expenditures in 1973)
gives the contrary result.[2]

Again, where consumption patterns differ markedly
between two countries, say Britain and China, a comparison of their GNPs is likely to differ significantly
according to whether the economist, in calculating a real
rate of exchange, adopts the patterns of expenditure of
one country or the other.

Having decided, somewhat arbitrarily, how to deal
with this perennial index-number problem in estimating
the particular change in real GNP, the economist has
recourse to a number of fairly obvious adjustments. If,
say, the apparent real growth in GNP happens to equal
the growth in the nation's population over the same
period, there is no cause for rejoicing since real GNP *per*

capita (roughly real income per capita) has remained the same. The economist may also be interested in technical progress, however, in which case he will want to estimate changes in GNP per working hour. Thus even though the economy as a whole is not performing well since, as a result of large-scale involuntary unemployment, per capita GNP is below that of an earlier year, technical progress as revealed by GNP per working hour could be taking place.

It may be noted in passing, however, that although such technical efficiency index calculated for women alone may be increasing, if the proportion of women in the workforce grew significantly over the period in question, the overall index of technical efficiency would be slowed down or could even fall. This is because the average real output per hour of women, although rising, is still much below that of men and so 'drags down' the overall average.

CONVENTIONAL RESERVATIONS ABOUT GNP ESTIMATES

Primary concern with the growth of GNP, or of per capita GNP, as an index of material improvement requires the economist to make allowance for some of the more relevant trends in the economy. If, for instance, the average number of hours per worker is voluntarily reduced over time, allowance has to be made for the value of the increased leisure enjoyed by the working population. Some further adjustment is needed in a dynamic economy inasmuch as the nature of the work itself alters over time in many occupations and can be more congenial to the worker or less so. Such changes in net satisfaction arising from changes in working conditions are difficult to determine and measure.

Similarly it is difficult to measure qualitative differences in consumer goods. For a particular class of goods, say radio sets, performance may have improved radically over the last two decades along with a fall in their prices relative to other goods. The relative fall in their prices properly enters the price index, but attribution by an economist of some addition to GNP in token of this improved performance involves arbitrary and possibly controversial assumptions. The contrary tendency, a decline over time in satisfaction from other consumer goods, say a loss in flavour of fruits and vegetables which results from modern methods of production, storage and transport associated with large-scale agribusiness, poses similar problems. Needless to remark, the introduction into the economy of novel consumer goods and the withdrawal of other goods also exercise the ingenuity of the economist while extending the penumbra of doubt about the validity of adjusted GNP estimates.

The valuation of the products and services that are provided, not by the private sector but by the government sector, creates additional misgivings in the conscientious economist. For whereas there is *prima facie* case for the assumption that a willingness to pay £100 for an item in a shop is evidence that the item is worth at least £100 to the individual, there can be no such assumption that a man obliged to pay £100 more in taxes values the additional government services to him (if any) as worth at least £100. For in the latter case he is not free to choose, and though he may well appreciate the range of services provided by the government, he himself may not want them all or he may want them in amounts other than those made available to him.[3]

Again, government agencies may be overstaffed and the efficiency of a part of their personnel low when compared with that in private industry and commerce. Yet the cost to citizens of the government's output enters into the estimate of GNP as the value of public services on a par with the value of the goods they buy from the private sector of the economy.

Further reservations arise from the fact that useful services are performed for the nation which are undertaken neither by the government nor by the market, the more familiar instance being the services rendered by housewives. It is possible, nevertheless, to make some crude adjustment for these unpriced services by multi-

plying the estimated hours worked by the nation's housewives during the year by an average hourly market rate
for domestic services.

Although such estimates are often attempted, they are
not in fact included in the GNP figure. Nor are estimates
for other services such as gardening or home repairs done
by members of the family as an alternative to hiring
others. The best excuse for excluding such inter-family
services is the belief that their real value does not alter
much over short periods and, therefore, the calculated
year-to-year *changes* in GNP do not (on that account at
least) convey a misleading impression. With respect to
the services of housewives at least, this belief is variance
with developments over the last three decades or so, with
implications for the estimated changes in GNP which we
consider below.

HOW CERTAIN IS THE SECULAR GROWTH IN
THE WEST OF REAL INCOME?

Notwithstanding such sources of error and bias in computing the value of the nation's GNP, most economists
believe that when used as an index from year to year the
figure does provide a fair idea, at least not a misleading
idea, of comparative economic performance. Over short-
ish periods of say two to three years such errors and
biases are unlikly to vary wildly, at any rate not to the
extent that would vitiate the propriety of year-to-year
comparisons.

Plausible though such assumption is for short-period
comparisons of GNP, it is not so for longish periods. For
economists and others who are interested in the larger
question — whether the affluent societies of the West are
better off in some significant sense than they were say
thirty, fifty or a hundred years ago — closer attention has
to paid not only to the sources of error and bias
mentioned above but also to other and more potent
sources of error and bias.

It should be manifest by now that the ultimate ingred-

ient of GNP or 'real' income is not some compound of
tangible goods such as steel bars and cabbages. As economists are at pains to point out in elementary texts,
although the value of steel bars and cabbages enter GNP,
it is the value of the *services* provided by steel bars and
cabbages that has to be entered as real income. And
since people themselves, as potential consumers, will
decide whether or not a particular item has a value, and
if so what value, it follows that in the last resort the value
of the goods produced by the economy is *subjectively*
determined by people according to the satisfactions they
anticipate from their use or possession.

In the event, then, rather than follow an older tradition which draws a distinction between economic and
non-economic goods, it is more appropriate to talk of the
value that economic activity can contribute to society's
overall well-being. Thus the goods produced by economic
activity, as measured roughly by GNP, are to be thought
of only as a component of the sum of satisfactions
enjoyed by society. But they are not a separable and
additive component. In a dynamic economy in particular,
the changing methods of production and the innovations
continually being adopted interact with and permeate the
style of living, making life for ordinary people either
more or less wholesome and enjoyable. As a result, it is
far from certain that the economic growth registered by
economists over, say, the last fifty years in any of the
countries of the West should be accepted even as a rough
measure of the growth in 'living standards'. Being the
denizens of a quantomaniac society, we could easily be
also the victims of a statistical hallucination.

HOW EASY IS IT TO OVERESTIMATE REAL GROWTH?

Let us turn first to the increased participation of women
in the workforce over the last thirty years, which has
increased output in the private and public sectors of the
economy and to that extent has increased the estimated
growth in real GNP and also in per capita real income. A

good part of this apparent contribution to the GNP statistics is, in an economic sense, fictitious. For while the services that women now provide for industry and commerce continue to add to the value of GNP, the concomitant reduction of services they would otherwise have provided in their homes — which on proper economic accounting would enter as a deduction from the nation's aggregate of finished goods — is ignored in the GNP computation.

We might amuse ourselves by imagining a somewhat ironic situation in which all wives sally forth each day from their homes in order to work in local factories that produce domestic labour-saving appliances. With their take-home pay these women are just able to furnish their homes with the latest in micro-computer gadgetry so that housework has become no more than a minute's work necessary to set the switches. These erstwhile housewives now work exactly the same hours in the factory as they used to do in the home with the old-fashioned appliances. Clearly, no less work is done in the new situation and no more finished household services are produced. Yet as compared with the old situation GNP will have increased by as much as the annual (pre-tax) incomes these women now earn. (Even with this simplified example, however, some adjustments are needed. On the one hand, there is some increase in real income equal to the taxes they now pay — in effect a transfer of their income to others — and to the measure of their preference for working in the factory rather than in the home. On the other hand, there may be some diminution as a result of neglect of home and children.)

Second, since public goods tend to be overvalued as compared with those produced by the private sector, as explained earlier, and since the output of the public sector over the last thirty years has grown appreciably as a component of GNP, it follows that the real growth of GNP over the period will be overestimated. Moreover, insofar as productivity gains in the government sector continue to lag behind those being made in the rest of the economy, while the salaries of civil servants tend to follow those in the private sector, this differential cost of government services increases over time which acts to overstate further the real growth in GNP.

Third, military expenditure which is the largest single item in public expenditure, although it is also subject to the above tendencies, raises another interesting question. Allowing that real military expenditure per capita has grown enormously since the turn of the century, should proper economic accounting include it as an increasing component of per capita real income? Some competent economists answer in the affirmative. The nation, they argue, has collectively chosen to use an increasing part of its total resources on defence rather than on other goods. It may therefore be inferred that, say, an additional $100 billion spent by the USA on defence is worth more to that nation than any other collection of civilian goods that could have been produced with this expenditure of $100 billion.

Let us concede that the nation has agreed that there is no better way of spending this $100 billion than on military defence. Yet such a fact is not to the purpose. For if the potential enemies of the USA had not increased their military strength, the USA (we could suppose) would have chosen instead to spend the $100 billion on civilian goods. It follows that the nation judged it necessary to make this sacrifice of $100 billion of civilian goods simply in order to restore the military *status quo ante*. And it certainly does not follow that the people of the USA are made any better off by this $100 billion of expenditure than they were *before* the potential enemy had increased his military strength.

Such additional military expenditures as are deemed necessary by the people of the USA are, properly speaking, regrettable. For in the absence of untoward developments abroad, the material standard of living in the USA would indeed be higher. To take a limiting case, if the whole of the real increase of GNP of $500 billion over a decade had to spent entirely on military goods in the endeavour to maintain the nation's external security, it would be misleading to conclude that the people of the

USA were enjoying a higher standard of living — enjoying, that is, additional goods to the value of $500 billion. Like remarks apply to additional expenditures over time required simply in order to maintain a given standard of internal security. Clearly, to the extent that, notwithstanding additional expenditures on external and internal security, apprehension of increased vulnerability grew over the period, an economic calculation of real living standards would require a deduction from GNP of sums greater than these defence expenditures.

Third, an increasingly significant source of error arises from the global exploitation of irreplaceable resources. A useful definition of 'net income' once proposed by Sir John Hicks is 'that level of expenditure over the period which would maintain capital intact'. On this definition net capital accumulation is part of income whereas net capital decumulation implies that, over the period, expenditure exceeds the resultant income. Thus, ignoring the net capital decumulation (or overestimating net capital accumulation) will overstate net income on this definition.

If, now, the total stock of capital is taken to include not only man-made capital but 'nature-made' capital such as fossil fuels, mineral reserves, ocean fisheries, tropical forests, and so on, it is entirely possible for current rates of global consumption to be reducing the stock of nature-made capital faster than the stock of man-made capital is increasing, which implies that we are currently consuming beyond our real income — in effect, eating into the total capital we have inherited to the detriment of our future and our children's future. Without going so far, however, real income is in general overstated where net reductions in nature-made capital is ignored in GNP calculations.[4] Clearly, the greater the variety of natural assets included in total capital — and they could include water reserves, wetlands, areas of wilderness, wildlife, and natural beauty — the greater the overestimation of real income.

A fourth factor related to the preceding one is the propensity of modern industry and its products to pollute air, soil and water and generally to degrade the environment, which clearly acts to reduce real income below the official figures. If, to begin with, nothing is done to curb the industrial overspill which damages the health and amenity of people, GNP is overstated to the extent of the cost of the damage that is borne — this being the value of the 'bads' that accompanies the production and distribution of the goods.

If, instead, all or part of some pollutant is in fact reduced over a given period, the cost of doing this has to be set against the benefit. But this does not necessarily happen. True, the benefit of pollution-removal is real enough *after* the pollution has occurred. Yet there is no such benefit if we compare the new pollution-reduced situation with an earlier one *before* the pollution began: no adjustment for benefits need be made then in comparing the new GNP with this earlier GNP estimate. But what of the additional costs of pollution-control newly incurred which did not exist in the earlier situation? It makes a difference if the pollution abatement is undertaken by private industry without subsidy rather than by the government.

If, for example, the damage arising over the period from a new form of water pollution is wholly reduced by the industry responsible, its expenditure on water purification raises the unit cost, and therefore also the price, of the industry's finished product. Such a price increase, however, is entered along with other price increases in the economist's price index which is used to deflate the nominal growth of GNP to a real figure. In this way the additional costs of restoring amenity are effectively subtracted from any estimated real increase in GNP.

On the other hand, if the government itself undertakes to purify the water polluted by the private industry, the expenditure appears in the national accounts as the provision of a public good for which, via taxation, there is a corresponding reduction in the production of private goods. No necessary change in GNP occurs for this reason. But the important difference is this: the prices of the polluting industry's products are in this case *not* raised and therefore their contribution to GNP is not deflated as it should be.

Put in a different way, the services of the water-purification plant is correctly conceived as an additional *intermediate* good whose cost raises the price of the industry's finished good to the community. And this is indeed what takes place when the industry itself finances the water-purification plant without government subsidy. Where the government undertakes the project, however, it appears as a *finished* (public) good, for which no correction is made — as a result of which the growth of GNP over this longer period is overstated.

In passing, the analogy between this case and the military expenditure case may be noted. Taken over a longish period of time, expenditures by the government in combating new forms of pollution and disamenity fit comfortably into the category of 'regrettables'. For the resources that are increasingly directed into the provision of anti-pollution goods serve only to restore and maintain standards of amenity. An increase in the real expenditure on such 'goods' over time is in fact an increase in costs, one which takes effect as a commensurate reduction in economic resources that would otherwise have been available for the production of additional consumption and capital goods.

THE TEMPTATIONS TO SURRENDER TO CYNICISM

The above comments, I imagine, will be acceptable to many economists. Indeed, since a number of specialists spend much time sifting and refining the raw data, official real income figures may yet appear in which allowances are made, among other things, for such sources of overestimation. But if the arguments in the preceding section are valid, we can hardly stop there. For the essential logic used to reject the notion that additional expenditures on external and internal defence and on public anti-pollution goods are (necessarily) contributions to real income can, in fact, be extended to cover all too many components of GNP. On inspection, that is, such components look less like contributions to finished goods (or goods 'wanted for their own sake') and more like regrettable or intermediate goods. In other words, they can be more, revealingly conceived as additional input cost rather than as additional output value.

A large part of the expenditures of modern government, which since the turn of the century, have grown enormously as a proportion of GNP, can reasonably be placed in this category. Rather than regarding government expenditure as a contribution to the value of finished goods produced by the economy, a large part may be classified as additional costs of administration, infrastructure and new agencies which are necessary to control and monitor a modern dynamic economy. For example, the growth in government expenditures on regulatory, rate-setting and conciliatory agencies are clearly a part of the increased costs of running industry; as also are the additional costs incurred in order to revise standards in the light of scientific discovery, to analyze some scores of thousands of products and by-products of industry and to disseminate their findings; as, again, are the greater expenditures on tax-collecting, on the police, on diplomacy and espionage, and so on.

But why stop at public expenditure. Looked at in historic perspective, many of the services provided in the private sector of the economy — provided by banks, by labour unions, by employment agencies, welfare agencies, travel agencies, by lawyers and accountants, by marriage bureaus and computer-dating services, by race-relations organizations and sex-advice clinics — were not needed in a more traditional society of small towns and villages. They come into being, and grow in importance, as population grows and becomes more mobile, as urban areas take on metropolitan dimensions and as the economy and mode of living become more complex. These agencies which spring up in response to individual bewilderment and to a need for expert guidance, information and comfort in a 'post-industrial' milieu may be regarded as forms of institutional lubricant necessary to the operation of the increasingly complex machinery of society — this complexity being an unavoidable by-product of technological progress.[5]

Also to be included as intermediate goods or inputs is that large and growing proportion of GNP on travel and commuting that is not enjoyed for its own sake — that, indeed, may be disliked — but is incurred simply as a means of reaching a destination. And in a civilization in which stress diseases are only too common, a good pro-portion of the burgeoning expenditure on vacations and tours may properly be included in this category as being conducive, if not necessary, to the continued functioning of the modern economy.

We can go further. Much the larger proportion of the costs of education, although more particularly higher education, is a form of current expenditure that — bearing in mind its predominantly vocational nature — is analogous to the part played by 'replacement investment' in maintaining the stock of physical capital. For this annual investment in higher education is likewise in-curred as an input in order to replenish the stock of skilled human capital, without which the running of a modern industrial economy is impossible.

What has been said of education can be extended to the information media. A large part of the country's expenditure on books, journals, newspapers, on radio and television, and more recently on home and business computers, has become necessary not only for vocational education, for coping with a mass of accumulating infor-mation, but also for effective participation in the eco-nomic, social and political activities of a high technology civilization. To that extent such expenditure is not that on final consumer goods but rather an inescapable cost of living in this civilization.

If these and other deficiencies in the conventional methods of estimating changes in GNP were recognized, and allowance made for them, the real standard of living in the West as compared with that of the other 'less developed countries' would look much less impressive. What is more, a corrected estimate of the rise in per

capita real income over the last fifty years in any of the
Western countries would be significantly smaller than
that derived from the conventional statistics, and could
possibly be negative.

Taking a longer look into the past only adds to one's
scepticism. With the collapse of a social life that in
Britain once centred in villages and small towns, the
search for new forms of diversion and solace produced
the music halls, the carnivals and the brass bands of the
Victorian and Edwardian eras. These were followed in
the inter-war period by the cinema and the radio, and in
the post-war era by stereophonics, television and computer games, supplemented by fantasy sex in erotic
magazines, in 'adult' theatre and videos. The affluent
society is now also liberally sprinkled with private and
public 'homes' and clinics designed to cope with the
rising incidence of individual distress and breakdown
arising from a 'lifestyle' fashioned by relentless technological progress. Emergency services proliferate. 'Hot-
Line' facilities cater for everything from drug-abuse and
post-abortion depression to suicidal/homicidal impulses
and homosexual loneliness.

It is difficult to call a halt to the train of instances of
technical and social innovations that, appearing at first
blush like contributions to a better standard of living,
turn out on reflection to be more like contributions to a
higher cost of living. So much of the nation's effort and
ingenuity are spent today in producing sophisticated
products and specialized services which cater, ultimately,
to those basic biological and psychological needs that —
it could be argued — were more easily and naturally met
in some of the pre-industrial civilizations.

NOTES

1. Textbooks rightly dwell on the difficulties of drawing a line
   between consumer goods and capital goods, which, however,
   need not detain us since wherever it is drawn the use of gross
   investment in GNP entails double-counting.

In passing I should emphasize the word 'roughly' above (main text) since replacement investment during the year (and 'pure' replacement seldom occurs) is usually more than, or less than, the sums set aside for amortization by public and private enterprises.

2. The inquisitive reader might like to consult Part VII of my *Introduction to Normative Economics* (Oxford University Press, 1981) for an appreciation of this seeming paradox, which has fascinated theoretical economists for two generations.

3. In this connexion, many economists continue to believe that in the *absence* of any government sector, the net national product — assuming it could be estimated exactly — would markedly under-state the value of all market goods inasmuch as the figure makes no allowance for 'consumer surplus', or the sums people would be willing to pay for the goods they buy above what they actually pay. This supposition is an error and arises from extending the concepts of partial-equilibrium analysis into a general-equilibrium context.

In general, the larger the set of goods being considered by the individual, the smaller, proportionally, is this consumer surplus. Once all the goods he buys are included, the most that the individual will pay for them all is exactly equal to his total expenditure, which, under familiar assumptions, is equal to his income.

4. A common belief among economists that the consumption of finite resources (whether optimal or not) is offset in value by the formation of other capital, is erroneous. Under familiar behaviour assumptions, no more than a fraction of the value of the finite resource is replaced, and this fraction could be negligible. For an analysis of this proposition, *see* my essay in Chapter 9 of *Theory for Economic Efficiency*, ed. by H. Greenfield *et al.* (The M.I.T. Press, 1979).

5. Moreover, to the extent that the citizen is less well served, to the extent that there is more crowding, more queuing, longer waiting periods, poorer service in the shops and generally less courtesy, more frustration and aggravation than there was, say, fifty years ago, these unregistered social costs have to be set against esti-mates of growth of GNP over that period.

PART III

INTRODUCTION

The rapid expansion of the public sector since the turn of the century is believed by liberal economists to have been inspired by muddled thinking among socialists who want to see a system of wasteful 'production for profit' replaced by central economic planning for 'the needs of the people' and who conceive of the state as an irresistible power for good when it is controlled by the right party — which is, of course, a party of the Left.

Inasmuch as such socialist aspirations are believed to be rooted in unworldliness and in intellectual error, quite a number of books have been written by well-known economists such as Von Mises, Hayek and Friedman with the object of revealing the self-regulating mechanism of the market which caters so admirably to the effective demands of consumers and, by contrast, the waste and inefficiency of centrally planned economies, to say nothing of the restriction on individual choice and the diminution of political freedoms.

While I concede that the continued expansion of the state since the Second World War threatens individual freedom, the notion that this development has much to do with socialist error is doubtful. At all events, I argue in Chapter 6 that technological progress is today the chief factor that, by creating unprecedented problems and conflicts, impels the public itself to demand increased government control and regulation.

In Chapter 7, I address myself to the twentieth-century myth that 'more is better'. To contradict the slogan, to assert instead that 'more is worse' is not to be taken with a grain of salt as being one of the habitual mutterings of a misanthrope or an intellectual snob — not, at least, when our concern is with the welfare of ordinary people enmeshed in the affluent society.

Though I enjoy a romp through this controversial area,

my excursion into it is limited by considerations of space. But I hope to convince the reader that there are grounds for the belief that all the popular policy goals of Western democracies — an increase in 'the goods things of life' (those found in the shops), a more equal distribution of income and wealth, increased mobility and travel opportunities, an expansion of education and also of the social services — all will tend to make life less enjoyable or will become necessary just because life will be less enjoyable.

Likewise, the assertion of technocrats that the 'revolution' in automation, computers, robots, will lighten our labours and so make our lives more leisurely and pleasant, may be taken as evidence either of their eagerness to be called upon to solve new social and environmental problems which they (inadvertently) create or else of their touching innocence about the biological and psychological needs of human beings.

In my last chapter, I touch upon the myths that are embodied in the 'adversary culture' of the West — prevalent among the Left and among academic intellectuals and scientists — that 'capitalism' or private enterprise or big business are institutions that are 'exploitive', wasteful, 'repressive' and are, indeed, responsible for most of our economic and social ills.

Although I do not deny the frustrations and vexations that arise from so many of the untoward features of our civilization, I do not attribute them to the economic system we call capitalism. Existing socialist economies do not look any more attractive than existing 'capitalist' ones. An ideal socialist system would perform no better than an ideal capitalist one.

The many uncongenial features that have accompanied the growth of mass affluence are, I contend in Chapter 8, to be attributed instead to the rapidity of technological innovation since the Second World War. In these historical circumstances, the tiresome phrases of economists and of political spokesman about the importance of economic growth in 'widening the area of choice' for the common man are also absurd.

There is also, in this last chapter, mention of the

uneasy myth we are apt to cling to in these ungodly days, that science and religion (when 'properly understood', of course) complement one another. Strange and uneasy, indeed, when it could hardly be more strikingly obvious that they are diametrically opposed — or, rather would be if religion took a stand on its faith. In fact, religion has surrendered ground to science ever since the Renaissance, and at an accelerating pace. Today, the authority of science has completely eclipsed that of religion. And if men are seen today to be chasing after newly contrived pop religions and religio-therapies, it is part of the reaction to the growing despair from living in a secularized society.

And this observation itself makes one wonder if the greatest myth of all today is the apparent belief that a metropolitan civilization of self-seeking and highly mobile atomistic families can somehow be expected to cohere, to continue as a free people sustained by economic and hedonistic opportunities alone; held together, that is, as a libertarian civilization, or at any rate a viable civilization, without respect for their leaders or their institutions, without a pride in their common origin or history, without a moral consensus and without transcendental faith or enduring sense of purpose.

6 The Road to Repression

OF CAPITALISM AND FREEDOM

The fundamental threat to freedom is the power to coerce, be it in the hands of a monarch, a dictator, an oligarchy, or a momentary majority. The preservation of freedom requires the elimination of such concentration of power to the fullest possible extent and the dispersal and distribution of whatever power cannot be eliminated — a system of checks and balances.

(Milton Friedman)

Liberal economists or, less ambiguously, libertarian economists have long regarded a competitive private-enterprise system not only as an economically efficient institution but also as one of the great bulwarks of liberty. This view has been eloquently argued by a number of outstanding economists in our own day. For instance, F.A. Hayek in his celebrated *Road to Serfdom* (1944) quotes Adam Smith as follows:

The statesman who should attempt to direct private people in what manner they ought to employ their capitals, would not only load himself with a most unnecessary attention, but assume an authority which could safely be trusted to no council whatever, and which would nowhere be so dangerous as in the hands of a man who had the folly and presumption to fancy himself fit to exercise it.

Elaborating on the nature of this danger, Hayek goes on to remark:

Once the communal sector, in which the state controls all the means, exceeds a certain proportion of the whole, the effects of its actions dominate the whole system. Although the state controls directly the use of only a large part of the available resources, the effect of its decisions on the remaining part of the economic system becomes so great that indirectly it controls almost everything. Where, as was for example true in Germany as early as 1928, the central and local

131

authorities directly control the use of more than half the national income (according to an official German estimate, then 53 per cent), they control indirectly almost the whole economic life of the nation. There is, then, scarcely an individual end which is not dependent for its achievement on the action of the state, and the 'social scale of values' which guides the state's action must embrace practically all individual ends.

Hayek might well have carried the argument a stage further. For the belief, popular among socialists, that in a democracy the state itself is in the last resort controlled by the electorate, or that a free press ensures the existence of an 'open society', is less than a half-truth. When one considers the sheer size of the modern nation-state, the control exercised by the electorate over the full range of activities of a government that absorbs close to (or more than) 50 per cent of the entire national product is limited to broad direction only. Its control of detail is remote and ineffectual. The continuing concern of the politically minded citizen is of necessity, then, directed in the main to contemporary bread-and-butter issues, on which issues politicians and political parties base their bid for office.

Thus, a bureaucracy that has come to embrace about half the entire economy, whose tentacles are spread wide in all directions, is not easily reformed, or even influenced, by a political party's brief tenure of office. States grow within states. There are groups within sub-committees within committees within sections within departments, the activities of which — the very existence of which — are unknown to the public and unsuspected by politicians. Under the general rubric of what is today known as R. and D. (research and development), for example (especially R. and D. associated with internal and external defence), projects are undertaken and experiments conducted which, were they known, would outrage the public.[1]

Be that as it may, the good fight against the persistent tendency towards government expansion never falters from lack of support.

Among the economists today who, through their

writings and speeches, have sought and continue to seek actively to arrest the growing encroachment of the power of the state on the diminishing private sector of the economy, perhaps the best known is Milton Friedman, who would readily affirm today what he wrote in his *Capitalism and Freedom* in 1962:

The kind of economic organisation that provides economic freedom directly, namely, competitive capitalism, also promotes political freedom because it separates economic power from political power and in this way enables the one to offset the other.

Declaring that *economic* freedom (in the sense of individual freedom to choose man-made goods) is best realized through competitive markets, Friedman goes on to observe that:

What the market does is to reduce greatly the range of issues that must be decided through political means, and thereby to minimise the extent to which government need participate directly in the game. The characteristic feature of action through political channels is that it tends to require or enforce substantial conformity. The great advantage of the market, on the other hand, is that it permits wide diversity.

Yet this same competitive private-enterprise system that extends economic freedom acts also to promote *political* freedom. For by removing the organization of economic activity from the control of political authority, the market eliminates this source of coercive power. It enables economic strength to be a check to political power rather than a reinforcement.

I confess that I am in sympathy with the broad sweep of this argument. Like most of my colleagues in the economics profession I am always ready to concede a presumption in favour of decentralized private enterprise and competitive markets unless convincing reasons to the contrary are adduced — as, of course, they sometimes can be when it comes to the introduction of a public good or the curbing of a public 'bad'. Although the operations of free markets and decentralized enterprise cannot of themselves prevent a gradual degradation of the quality of life or an erosion of moral values, they are surely more congenial to the exercise of effective economic and political freedom than is the concentration of economic power in the hands of giant corporations or, worse, in the hands of the state.

A NEGLECTED AVENUE OF INQUIRY

Chancellor Denis Healey's controversial plan to clamp down on tax evasion was given an unopposed second reading after an Opposition attack on it was defeated by 288 votes to 274. The Tories will keep up the pressure to tone down the powers of what have been scornfully dubbed 'Healey's secret police'.

Shadow Chancellor Sir Geoffrey Howe accused him in last night's debate of turning Britain into 'a kind of fiscal Lubianka' and complained about the way the announcement of the new powers had been slipped through 'on a dark Maundy Thursday' (when there were no morning newspapers being published the next day).

Mr Healey was obviously taken aback by the scale of the opposition to his plans. Some newspapers, he said, had 'conjured up Kafkaesque fantasies ... the sort of Tory-Trotskyism that is spawning in the damp cellars of the Carlton Club and Annabel's.'

(Daily Mail/The Times)

Nevertheless, in spite of the manifest resentment of ordinary citizens at the scale and frequency of government intervention, and in spite of the articulate apprehension of liberals everywhere, in spite even of the occasional resolutions of government spokesmen, the size of the public sector has continued to grow remorselessly in all Western countries since the turn of the century. As recently as the early 1930s, total US government expenditure (federal, state and local) barely amounted to 10 per cent of net national expenditure. By 1940 it had risen to 25 per cent; by 1950 to 29 per cent; and by 1970 to 42 per cent. Although it has not yet topped 50 per cent, the critical proportion beyond which, according to F.A. Hayek, the government 'controls indirectly the whole economic life of the nation', and although it is still far from the 60-per-cent share of the British government (which, according to Roy Jenkins, would make 'pluralism' difficult), it does seem to be moving in that direction.

The question which has, therefore, to be faced is whether — in addition to the impetus provided by the enthusiasm of planners and technocrats, and by the empire-building propensities of bureaucrats — there is in fact a secular tendency for government to expand at the expense of the private sector; in particular, whether this tendency is itself a consequence of rising levels of affluence.

Here, then, is a rich vein of inquiry that has too long been neglected. Its terms of reference may be expressed as follows. Does the process of economic growth itself cause both a diminution in the private sector of the economy and a diminution of individual liberty? Two things may be noticed about the wording of the question.

First, that an explanation in terms of economic growth does not preclude other, and possibly complementary, explanations. One of the most remarkable social phenomena of the post-war period is the re-emergence in the West of a veritable passion for equality, one that is marked by a growing impatience with privilege or authority whatever its source. The 'revolution of expectations' is transforming itself into what Daniel Bell has recently called the 'revolution of rising entitlements' — in effect, a revolution of mass sentiment expressing itself in the demand that the state provide and guarantee whatever discontented majorities or aggrieved minorities deem to be right and proper.

This phenomenon is not surprising. The extension of democracy along with the growth of affluence over that last 100 years has encouraged the spread of egalitarian sentiment. Indeed, the demand for the universal extension of opportunity to compete for the economic prizes — popular among the enlightened Establishment before the Second World War — has been transformed today into a demand to share in whatever economic prizes are won; a demand that is being met, however, not so much through direct income transfers but rather through burgeoning public expenditures on health, education and welfare services generally.

Such an explanation of events — in terms, that is, of

democratic and egalitarian forces — is not uncongenial to
the liberal mind since it offers hope for the future. The
good fight against persistent government enroachment
could hardly be waged with conviction unless it were
believed that this seeming trend could be checked, if not
reversed; that is, unless it were believed that the factors
making for more government are not decisive and need
not, in the last resort, prevail against the express desires
of that enlightened electorate which it is the task of the
good liberal economist to bring into being.

From this liberal perspective, at any rate, the public
sector in modern democracies grows in response to
popular egalitarian sentiment. And this sentiment, as it
happens, is linked to a strong preference for the government provision of specific services rather than for the
straightforward money transfers that are favoured by
liberal economists.

Complementary to this explanation in terms of egalitarian or populist sentiment is another; namely, that the
growth of government expenditures is directly facilitated
by the operation of existing progressive-income-tax
systems.

Although there is no necessary logical connexion
between economic growth and the growth of progressive
tax systems, there is indeed an historical connexion. In
Western democracies, at least, economic growth over the
last century has been accompanied by greater progression
of nominal income-tax rates. This phenomenon is one
that many economists regard as one of the direct causes
of government expansion. For a progressive-tax structure
in a growing economy enables the government to collect
over time an increasing *proportion* of the national
product, especially — as we now know to our cost — in
times of inflation. This is the result simply of moving
income-earners into higher tax brackets. From time to
time, of course, nominal tax rates are lowered. But they
are not lowered by enough to counteract the afore-
mentioned trend — a fact that makes it easier for governments to expand their activities.

For this reason alone there is a strong case for pro-

portional taxation, though one that will not be argued
here,[2] the point of these remarks being only to acknow-
ledge this characteristic property of the progressive-tax
structure in facilitating and encouraging government
expansion.

The second thing to notice about the wording of our
enquiry is the phrase 'a diminution of individual liberty'.
There is an obvious sense in which, as Friedman and
others have argued, any extension of government activity
at the expense of the private sector of the economy itself
reduces both the variety of choices open to the citizen
and the economic power at his disposal. But the implication of the phrase goes further than this. For, without
any significant increase in the government sector of the
economy, there can be substantial reductions in individual liberty arising directly out of repressive legislation.
What is more, this untoward development may well be
inescapable. It may be an unavoidable consequence of
the very direction and pattern of economic growth.

The fact that this possibility has not occurred to the
liberal economist must be attributed in some part to his
ideological commitment to that material progress which
he continues to regard, despite the accumulating evidence to the contrary, as a potent solvent of all social
frictions and personal frustrations. In some part also it is
due to the economist's habit of thinking about economic
growth in terms of a rise in the level, or flow, of an
abstract 'real' income. Even those liberal economists who
recognize the impact of economic growth on environmental amenity favour faster economic growth. To quote
Samuel Brittan's remark in his *Capitalism and the Permissive Society* 1973:

One very attractive way of taking out the fruits of faster economic
growth would be to make the working environment itself less
abrasive, even at the cost of some sacrifice in production. But to be
able to do this without making unacceptable inroads into real wages
we will require more rapid growth in our productive potential.

At best, economists have been satisfied to think about
economic growth in terms of more or better consumer

goods, which, it is said, 'expand the area of choice open to the individual'. As a result, they have paid too little attention to the particular kinds of technological innovation that, accompanying the process of economic expansion, have come to increase directly and indirectly the power and reach of the modern state.

In the event, I shall open the debate by propounding the thesis that there is indeed a direct relation between economic growth, or, more specifically, technological growth — this being, rather, the chief component and characteristic feature of modern economic growth — and the secular growth of government economic activity. I shall argue, in particular, that the concomitant decline in personal freedom is not only a corollary of this reduction in the private sector of the economy, it is the result also of conscious surrenders of personal rights and freedoms, this being the unavoidable reaction of society to the consequences of particular kinds of technology. If I am correct, it follows that the libertarian economist cannot consistently claim also to be a pro-growth economist.

A preliminary statement of my thesis is desirable at this stage. In general terms it may be affirmed that the slower the changes taking place in any civilized society and the greater the degree of moral consensus within it, the smaller is the scope for legislation. *Per contra*, the more rapid are the changes and the less the moral consensus, the greater is the amount of legislation required. Moreover, in such conditions, the resulting legislation, passed in haste and based (as it will be) on compromise and expediency, is likely to please few and disgruntle many. The latter statements are clearly descriptive of the political situation prevalent in most Western democracies. And a moment's reflection about its causes takes us to the heart of the matter.

Rapid economic development over the last century has been responsible not only for an unprecedented expansion of populations the world over but also (especially in the richer countries) for the growing mobility of their populations. Among the consequences have been a rapid increase in the size and crowdedness of urban areas and a continuing change in their composition. Moreover, the concomitant innovations in industrial processes and products that (measured by conventional indices) have multiplied real incomes in the West, have been productive also of powerful side effects which, for our purpose, can be divided into two overlapping categories: those which expose humanity to hitherto unknown dangers, and those adverse spillovers which, in modern nation-states, are continually translated into overt conflicts of interest. Both the dangers and the conflicts are, at best, contained by legislation, but generally at the expense of individual choice and, therefore, at the expense of individual freedom.

NEW SOURCES OF MUTUAL ANNOYANCE

I turn first to those innovations both of consumer goods and industrial processes that have incidental but direct and substantial effects on the well-being of others — effects which are known, in the economist's slang, as 'spillovers'. This analysis by economists turns on the concept of a divergence between social and market valuations and on methods for reducing this divergence.[3] In the light of my thesis, however, we must now take note of the propensity of these spillovers to augment the power of the state.

Grouping transport innovations, we can begin with the private automobile, which, apart from severely restricting the freedom of the would-be pedestrian, happens also to be a lethal weapon. Through its intensive use, Americans continue to kill off their countrymen at the rate of about 50,000 a year, in motor accidents alone, and to maim for life more than twice that number. Apart from that, its manifold nuisance value defies calculation. Society's half-hearted attempts to protect itself from the excesses of its beloved monster have already issued in a number of minor infringements of personal freedom. As automobiles continue to get in each other's way, they are subjected to closer regulation: to speed limits, parking prohibitions, one-way streets, no-entry precincts, and so on. Stricter controls on exhaust emissions and engine noise are on the way and, to enforce them, a variety of electronic devices and a growing army of traffic police.

The expansion of air traffic, both commercial and private, has also brought with it detailed regulatory legislation that can only grow over the future. The popularity of air travel, however, has other consequences. The promotion of mass tourism has already run into the incipient resentment of populations in the host countries, or of host regions within a country. Pressures on legislatures, local and national, to limit the freedom of people to travel where and when they wish, are becoming increasingly effective. Certainly, within the richer and more populated countries, motorized travel to national parks, wilderness areas and lake districts will soon have to be preserved from irrevocable spoliation. Traffic congestion is not, of course, the only issue. Owing to the so-called package revolution, legislation is being enforced in some countries, and is being contemplated in others, in the attempt to control the growing litter (much of it synthetic and non-degradable) on the streets, on the beaches, in parklands and in lakes and streams.

One might continue down the list of despoiling technology. For the post-war growth of our other motorized pastimes, involving the use of such things as motorcycles, speedboats, snowmobiles, private planes, has started a reaction among the more amenity-conscious citizenry — frequently identified by pro-growth economists as élitist middle-class kill-joys — which is manifestly on the increase, and which is sure to result in further restrictions on freedoms hitherto enjoyed by the motorized multitude.

The mounting concern over the last decade with air, water and soil pollution arising from new industrial processes and their products — in particular with the fouling of the air in metropolitan regions, with the destruction of forest, wetlands and everglades, with the dumping of sewage in estuaries and oil on the high seas, and with the wanton use of pesticides and chemical fertilizers — has led to an increase in controls in all countries, the import of which has not yet been fully appreciated. Certainly, in Britain they have excited little attention. In the United States, in contrast, the environmental interest has been vociferous enough to precipitate a rash of restrictive legislation, both state and federal. In 1970, for instance, the powerful Environmental Protection Agency was added to the existing number of federal regulatory bodies. Today, American businessmen no longer have the freedom to choose their most profitable type and scale of industrial plant, or its most profitable location.

In view of their excessive mobility and enterprise, it is not, of course, surprising that Americans are more conscious of these problems than other nationals. Some of them have also begun to perceive uneasily the shape of things to come. Thus, in the introduction to a recent report commissioned by Congress, economist Ronald Ridker wrote in 1972:

Conservation of our water resources, preservation of wilderness areas, protection of animal life threatened by man, restrictions on pollutant emissions, and the limitations on fertilizer and pesticide-use, all require public regulation. Rules must be set and enforced, complaints heard and adjudicated. True enough, the more we can find means of relying on the price system, the easier will be the bureaucratic task. But even if effluent charges and user fees become universal, they would have to be set administratively, emissions and use metered, and fees collected. It appears inevitable that a larger proportion of our lives will be devoted to filling in forms, arguing with the computer or its representative, appealing decisions, waiting for our case to be handled, finding ways to evade or move ahead in the queue. In many small ways, everyday life will become more contrived.

THE GREAT PAY SCRAMBLE

Let me now be rash enough to insinuate my thesis into an area of current controversy among economic specialists, the genesis of the new inflation. Since my leisurely reflections on this topic have already been published elsewhere,[4] I shall confine myself here to tracing a connexion between the shape of economic growth and the associated change of institutions in the West on the one hand, and on the other, the unparalleled scale of current pay claims that appears to be making it all but impossible for governments not to intervene actively, and continually, in industrial relations.

First let me bring to mind those innovations in transport, communication and industrial plant that have increased the size and economic power of both corporations and labour unions, national and multinational. There are some economists who choose to believe that the American economy is no less competitive today than it was fifty years ago, and on some kinds of definition this can be held to be true. But despite the growth of wealth and population, there are certainly fewer industrial firms today and, what is more significant, the larger corporations are very much larger than those of fifty years ago, whether measured in terms of value added, of capital used or of number of employees. Their power to influence voters and governments to support policies favourable to the corporations' business — through the buying up of advertizing space or time, through highly organized lobbies, and through scarcely concealed bribes to journalists, labour leaders and public-office holders — is too well known to require documentation. Nor need one waste time instancing the methods used by aggressive labour unions to intimidate individual workers and to bring pressure to bear on smaller labour unions that threaten their monopoly.

This growth of national monopolies on each side of industry has strengthened the propensity of both capital and labour to conspire against the public by raising production costs. It is a propensity that has been aggravated in the last two or three years by an unprecedented clamour for more money by the working populations in all Western countries. Owing to improved statistical techniques and to the employment of high-speed computers — owing also to the spread of news media and to the post-war surge of material expectations, itself inspired by the growth gospel and encouraged by government pronouncements — workers in all occupations have now become hypersensitive to movements in their real wages and to their position in the pay structure. The ordinary citizen having been fed on the pap of 'rising expectations' for almost a generation, no group today suffers an actual reduction in its real pay without a deep sense of grievance and, currently, without continuing action to recover and advance its real earnings — even when, for the economy as a whole, some (temporary) decline in real standards may be unavoidable. Although economists are fully aware of this *de facto* intransigence of the working population, and have to work it into their traditional fiscal and monetary theories, it is a phenomenon quite without parallel.

Unfortunately, at the very time that workers have become acutely conscious of movements in their real and relative earnings, they have also become aware of their collective power to inflict injury on their industry and, more important, to impose inconvenience or even hardship on local or national communities. Since developments in communication have been such that management, representing all the firms of 'the industry' in question, negotiates with labour leaders representing all workers in that industry, the most likely outcome is one that concedes the bulk of the wage claims, even if this entails a rise in the prices of the industry's outputs.

The likelihood of this sort of solution is stengthened in conditions of near-full employment, and of upward wage and price drift, that have largely prevailed since the Second World War. For if, in any important economic activity, industrial conflict looks imminent (or if any existing dispute is beginning to drag on), democratic governments, with their eyes always on the next election, are tempted to intervene.

Industrial peace in such cases generally entails concessions to labour. Since wage settlements, in one economic sector after another over the last few years, have invariably been in excess of productivity increases, prices have continued to move up. What is more, the resulting inflation becomes self-generating inasmuch as each wage settlement triggers off the pay claims of others whose positions in the pay structure are thereby disturbed.

Up to 1979 these developments culminated in rates of inflation that were causing alarm and despondency in Britain and other countries.[5] Given the existence of the welfare state and the commitment of all political parties to the 'full employment' objective, it seems highly unlikely that monetary and fiscal policies alone will suffice, over the foreseeable future, to maintain price stability. As events are moving, such policies look to be made subordinate and ancillary to an extension of price and wage controls. Even if my interpretation of these events is inadequate or mistaken, the tacit conspiracy against the public interest by capital and labour in the chief industries — a conspiracy that is one of the institutional outcomes of economic growth — is sure to strengthen the role of the central government as broker, as mediator and, in the last resort, as the wielder of countervailing power which, in the last desperate resort, may take a form that creates massive unemployment.

A FUTURE WORLD OF MORAL ANXIETY

The direction of current research in modern medicine is such as to make certain decisions increasingly painful and, indeed, given the trend towards a dissolution of traditional values, more difficult both at the personal and at the community level. In consequence, the government will be called upon to play a yet larger role in the social control of medicine. At least three trends are discernable which look as if they will culminate in increased government intervention: (1) the growing dependence of the medical profession upon expensive machines for diagnosis and treatment, (2) continuing improvements in the techniques of organ transplants and in those for preserving people in a non-sentient state for indefinite periods, and (3) the progress being made by research in RNA and DNA — the acid substances that store and pass on as heredity the blueprint for production of proteins by the cell.

Concerning (1), it may be assumed that physicians will want to invest in the new machines, for they believe (rightly) that their competence will be judged by the impressiveness of the equipment on display in their offices or clinics. Once bought, however, doctors will be under strong financial temptation to make maximum use of them, and they will, moreover, become increasingly dependent on them over time. With this development, a system of private medicine is more likely over the near future to threaten the private citizen with inordinate medical expenses[6] and, in consequence, to induce him to favour an extension of state medicine.

Another implication of this same development is that something akin to moral decisions have now to be made by medical staffs in hospitals where, because of their exhorbitant price, there are not always enough lung or kidney machines available for all patients who may benefit from their use.

Trends (2) and (3) also entail moral decisions of this nature. The enthusiasm of some surgeons for organ transplant operations has, according to press reports, led to the premature removal of the vital organ. Recently, for example, the victim of a motor accident was discovered to be still alive during the removal operation. So long as 'fresh' corpses are required by emergency wards, permission has to be sought from the close relations of the accident victims. Since it is now obvious that the information they receive should not come from the medical men who are anxious to exercise their skill in transplant operations, procedural rules will have to be formulated and enforced. Again, since medical evidence of death can be associated with the cessation of heart, lung or brain activity, there must also be criteria for determining whether or not a person is 'really' dead; whether and for how long to keep alive a person in a dormant state of being (a 'human vegetable'); or whether, and for how long, to keep a person alive when there is little hope of releasing him from continuous suffering, or when there is practically no hope of his ever enjoying life again. Thus, disturbing moral problems are raised by advances in modern medicine whose resolution, however, cannot be left to the discretion of the medical profession — least of all, at a time of eroding moral consensus.[7] In the last resort the rules will be shaped through the political process, and their application enforced through government agencies.

We can, finally, imagine the public consternation as scientists begin to uncover the secrets of the genetic code. Discoveries enabling them to breed clones[8] or, more potent still, to influence the genetic composition of human offspring, or to control it in 'test tube' babies — so that, among other possibilities, highly superior or inferior beings could be bred or, alternatively, animal or human beings that are 'freaks' in that they are highly specialized for particular purposes — may seem far away just now. But there can be no doubt that scientific research is moving in that direction. The moral problems to be faced would be painful, particularly if it were also feared that some other government, or group of scientists or fanatics, were planning to use the findings of such research for sinister ends. In the circumstances, only the most far-reaching powers of investigation and control wielded by governments acting in concert would suffice to allay such fears.

A moment's reflection will confirm that these are not idle fantasies. The most sensible course of action for mankind, it might be agreed, would be to prohibit further research in this dangerous area. But in the world of today international approval and operation of such a ban would be difficult on both political and 'scientistic' grounds. The import of the latter term has reference to the ideological presumption in favour of untrammelled scientific discovery, plus an unquestioned superstition that scientific freedom and personal freedom are closely intertwined. These are reinforced by broad humanitarian appeals whenever the public becomes uneasy about their possible social implications. The 'good' uses of the research in question are always stressed; the sufferings of some people who might benefit are continually emphasized. Thus it was in the recent decision of the British government to permit microbiologists and other scientists to continue their experiments in creating new mutations of bacteria — provided, of course, 'proper safeguards' were observed. And so the research goes on until substances and instruments of fearsome potential come into being within societies peopled by imperfect beings, among which there is, alas, no shortage of fanatic or criminal elements.

A SECRET FILE ON EVERYBODY

Scarcely anyone who was involved in the operations — bugging phones, breaking into houses, slipping LSD to unsuspecting bar patrons, planning assassination attempts, undermining governments — seems to have wondered whether he was doing anything wrong. The values of the men who operated in the shadowy underground world were summed up by William C. Sullivan, for ten years the head of the FBI's domestic intelligence division: 'Never once did I hear anybody, including myself, raise the question: "Is this course of action ... lawful, is it legal, is it ethical or moral?" We never gave any thought to this line of reasoning, because we were just naturally pragmatic.'

(Time Magazine)

Let us now consider some instances of those innovations in which the element of increasing hazard is the more immediate factor in the reduction of individual liberty. We may begin, arbitrarily, with a glance first at those developments, based either on microfilm or computer technology, which have vastly facilitated the storage, the processing, and the retrieval of information. Such developments have provided corporations and governments with inviting opportunities for extending the range of inquiry about their employees, their customers or the public at large.

As Jacques Ellul has observed in his *Technological Society* (1965), if a thing is technologically feasible, a use for it will sooner or later be discovered: 'Invention is the mother of necessity'. It is now becoming technically possible, and not too costly, for a government in an industrially advanced country to store information on the economic and political activities of all its citizens, and to exchange such information with other governments. We can, according to Ellul's generalization, confidently anticipate the phenomenon.

Although any overt scheme designed to extend the detail and coverage of information about the private lives of citizens would be viewed with alarm by the public, it would not be at all difficult to rationalize in the name of efficiency, and even in the name of humanity, as, for example, enabling assistance to be forthcoming more expeditiously to any victim of accident or hardship, or as a powerful aid in the detection and combating of crime or fraud. In view of the phenomenal growth in crime since the Second World War and the increasing danger it poses for society — about which more anon — it is not likely that such measures will be successfully resisted.

Apart from its existing uses by the police and the military, and its prospective uses indicated above, the need for more comprehensive dossier systems will grow with the economy's increasing dependence on the complex machines used in the control of modern plants. Computers, for example, perform such vital functions today as guiding missiles and airliners, and controlling the operation of steel and chemical plants. Their employment also in the operation of telephone exchanges or in the provision of other public utilities such as gas, water and electricity supply is sure to grow over the future. Since, in the interests of economy, a single plant can be made to serve a vast metropolitan area, a breakdown (or even a serious error in the operation) of such machines is exceedingly costly and could be disastrous. The same might be said of much simpler devices. Just imagine the consequences of a failure of the fail-safe device controlling the sequence of traffic lights in a large city!

Recognition of these new hazards must, of necessity, produce a system of closer checks and tighter controls on the personnel employed in the day-to-day management, maintenance and repair of such machines, a system which for its effective enforcement will come to depend, among other things, on the family histories and detailed psychological knowledge of the personnel in question. The intimate knowledge required to implement these neces-

sary precautions will increasingly be provided by specialized agencies, public or private, having highly developed
methods of prying into the private lives of ordinary
citizens. The extreme distaste with which, today, such
developments are regarded by liberals cannot, however,
prevent their continued growth. Indeed, the compilation
of such personal histories will be facilitated by the co-
operation of those citizens whose employment opportunities come to depend upon the availability of such
records.

LOW PROBABILITY HIGH-CONSEQUENCE RISKS

In this category appear those risks falling on the public
that arise from the day-to-day applications of science to
industry. Economic 'progress' in chemicals and synthetics, and in the food and drug industry, is being made in a
state of virtual ignorance.[9] Not only have we practically
no knowledge of the probability of any particular risk
occuring but for the most part we know nothing either of
the nature or of the extent of the damage that could be
associated with the production of the synthetic in question. The world simply has had no previous experience of
it, and the experiments, if any, to which it has been
subjected are perforce limited. Thus, although it is conceivable (though hardly likely) that the full range of
adverse consequences, and the probability distribution of
each of them, will come to light in the course of time for
each new substance and each combination of substances,
the social problem is that of creating or adapting institutions to cope with the dangers to which people are being
currently exposed.[10]

Slowly and haltingly, we are beginning to realize the
dangers that abound. Every so often — and sometimes,
as in the Thalidomide case, more by luck than by sys-
tematic investigation[11] — some new synthetic, drug or
food additive comes under official suspicion and, after
some preliminary inquiry, it is withdrawn from the
market. Sometimes the damage already wrought is

irrevocable;[12] sometimes not. What is certain, however, is that thousands of new drugs and synthetics come on to the market each year, a vague, persistent and growing threat to our health and survival.

Explicit forms of safety assurance are, of course, also being demanded in the USA by other government agencies, risk assessment being a major component in their current decisions. The recent Toxic Substances Control Act mandates that all chemicals (more than 3,000) be tested for carcinogenicity, mutagenicity, teratogenicity and other effects. The difficulties are immense. Extension of results from animal experiments to humans introduces a high level of uncertainty.[13]

Clearly, vital public decisions are being made under conditions in which analysis, dominated as it often is by a large element of uncertainty, cannot be rational. In some instances it is hardly a question of setting confidence intervals, for virtually nothing is known of a new substance or technology except the fears of some scientists of the possibility of a variety of calamities.[14] What, for example, is the risk that some malignant man-made bacterium will escape from a micro-genetic engineering laboratory and spread a disease against which men and animals have no natural defences, and against which modern medicine — within the relevant time span — would be powerless? Perhaps not too great just at present. But as the number of even very small risks of precipitating an irreversible or earth-crippling catastrophe continue to accumulate year by year — and some risks are far from small — the passage of time brings us closer to a near certainty of some such catastrophe.

Obviously, there can be very little individual choice in respect of the many new hazards of this sort arising from post-war innovations. Nor is there the remotest prospect of the market transmuting these collective choices — whether they are made explicitly or (in default of an explicit decision) implicitly — into individual choices. Whatever the nature and extent of the risk in question, such a risk is *involuntary* for the individual.

It may be argued that even where the degree of risk is

known, and it is clearly explained to the public, people perceive the danger to be larger than it actually is; worse, that when the degree of risk is not known, or when the public disbelieves the estimates of scientists, the risk may be exaggerated out of all proportion. Yet the economist, sticking to his last, is constrained by his evaluative criterion to accept as the only relevant data the valuation that each individual taken singly places on each good or bad including, of course, involuntary risk.

From this brief consideration of the public's growing awareness of the proliferation of hazards, large and small, local and global, that has taken place since the Second World War, two main conclusions follow. First and more obvious, the degree of public anxiety has increased, is increasing and will almost certainly continue to increase. In the circumstances, one should hesitate to accept the affirmation of growth-men that, over the post-war period, technological advance has on balance improved the human condition; that simply because of the availability of more market goods the general sense of well-being has grown in spite of public anxiety and trepidation.

The second conclusion emerges from the first and also from the fact that spillovers, old and new, produce conflicts of interests within the community between beneficiaries and 'maleficiaries' — as between government and industry, between consumers of polluting goods and the victims of such pollution, between particular industries (sometimes supported by government) and segments of the public, between ecologists and technocrats, between environmentalists and blue-collar workers.

Both these facts — the public's growing unease at the expanding horizon of hazard and the inevitable conflicts engendered by the hazards in question — tend to activate public demand for more government control and more detailed legislation, so diminishing further the prospect of a reduction in the power of government and an increase in individual freedom.

THE TECHNO-MILITARY SPIRAL

Let me now turn to a more obvious source of danger: the upward trend in military expenditures the world over. In 1913, US national defence expenditure was about 0·7 per cent of national expenditure. By 1940 it was 2 per cent. By 1950 it had grown to 7·5 per cent, and by 1970 it was over 10 per cent (or $84 billion, valued in 1974 dollars). This trend in defence expenditure is directly related to economic growth via the technical innovations that maintain its momentum. It is not, therefore, the result merely of military ambitions, or of administrative laxity, or of financial opportunism, or corruption in high places. The arms race between the powers, especially that between the 'superpowers', the USA and the USSR, does not take the form of accumulations of military hardware or of expanding military personnel. It takes the form of massive investment in developing and producing more expensive and deadlier weapons. For every weapon of offensive capability there is soon designed a weapon for defensive capability, the response to which is a yet more destructive offensive weapon, and so on. In the words of Charles Schultze, an American scholar in this field:

continually advancing technology and the risk aversion of military planners, therefore, combine to produce ever more complex and expensive weapons systems and ever more contingencies to guard against.[15]

Without technological progress, that is, these huge expenditures on research and development for the production of yet more complex and lethal weapons could not continue to spiral upwards.

The consequent rise in the level of general anxiety, though subversive of social welfare, may not seem directly relevant to my thesis. But this spiral of self-sustaining research inevitably produces scientific secrets of value to enemy agents. The resulting fears, real or imaginary, of ubiquitous enemy intelligence will go far to sanction the use of special powers for counterespionage

activities, including powers to investigate the private lives
not only of government employees but of every resident
in the country. There is precious little a government,
even a liberal democratic government, cannot do today in
the name of 'national defence' or 'military necessity'.

In sum, technological progress over the foreseeable
future will produce increasingly sophisticated and lethal
weapons, the secrets of whose operating principles and
construction, it is believed, must on no account be
allowed to fall into the hands of a hostile power. For
upon them, it can be plausibly argued, depends the
effective defence, if not the survival, of the nation. It
follows that the private activities and, in times of emergency or fear, the declared beliefs of private citizens, will
come under scrutiny and restriction.

TECHNOLOGY IN THE SERVICE OF CRIME

From external security, let me turn to internal security,
and recall to mind the alarming trend in crime statistics.
Notwithstanding the cherished beliefs of liberals and
humanists, the growth in the West of material abundance
— accompanied as it has been by a vast extension of state
welfare services, in particular by an extension of edu-
cational opportunities — has not, in the event, brought
about the anticipated decline in criminal activity. Quite
the contrary; crime has grown without interruption since
the end of the Second World War.

There is, of course, a temptation to explain this
unhappy trend also in terms of economic growth, with
perhaps special reference to the contemporary accent on
material status and on 'the good things of life', and the
concomitant neglect of traditional values; to explain it
also in terms of the decline of moral constraints[16] resulting from the diffusion of secular education, both formal
and popular. But I shall resist this temptation here. It is
enough to remark that the economic growth of the last
two centuries has had the incidental effect of expanding
the opportunities and the facilities for a life of crime. The

rapid enlargement of town and city in the nineteenth century can be traced back to the agricultural revolution and the Enclosure Acts of the eighteenth century, which broke up hundreds of small farm communities throughout the land. A succession of innovations in communication, in transport, in sanitation and in the provision of public utilities transformed the new industrial and commercial centres into huge urban agglomerations that sometimes ran to hundreds of square miles, the breeding grounds for hordes of petty criminals and thugs. They are ideal also for the operation of large criminal organizations. Against the anonymity and endless swirl of motorized humanity, their movements are difficult to detect. After some daring robbery or brutal crime, which today nearly always depends upon the fast get-away car (one of the great modern innovations), the criminal can hide for weeks within the big city by moving at short notice from one area to another, or within the hour he can be on a commercial airliner or private plane on his way to foreign parts.

However, what is more pertinent to my thesis is not the increase in the incidence of crime that has been facilitated by economic growth, but the power conferred on organized crime by technological innovation. It is by now abundantly clear that continued scientific research produces not only more expensive and complex missile systems or deadlier rays, gases and bacteria; it also produces critical simplifications in the design of smaller thermonuclear or bacteriological bombs that place them increasingly within the capacity of the smaller and less politically stable nation-states — and also within the capacity of the modern multinational criminal organization.

At a time when criminals and political fanatics — their effectiveness multiplied by swift travel, radio communication, 'bugging' and other devices — are becoming more active in intimidating the public by the kidnapping and the torture or murder of hostages, the fears instilled in the ordinary citizen are keener by his recognition also of the increased vulnerability of the large city or conurbation in which he dwells. For, as indicated earlier, in order to avail itself of the economies of large-scale production, the population of a city or of a whole region has come to depend increasingly upon a single source for its water supply, for its sewage disposal and for its electricity supply — this versatile source of power itself operating a host of subsidiary services vital to the functioning, indeed the survival, of the city or region.

Quite apart from the risk of a breakdown in one of these vital services,[17] one has to reckon today with the growing likelihood of their sabotage or attempted sabotage by criminal or urban guerrilla groups. The anxieties created by the apprehension of such hazards will issue inevitably in an extension of police powers. For the desire for security exceeds the desire for freedom; indeed, security is a precondition of freedom. Once the millions of people crowded into the cities begin to realize just how helpless and exposed they have become, there will be little resistance to police telephone-tapping, to closer monitoring of international and perhaps also internal travel, to the surrender of more arbitrary powers of search and arrest and, above all, to the pervasive surveillance and control that become more effective as scientific progress is made in chemical and other methods of identifying, tracing and incapacitating people. [18]

The last item under this heading, the peacetime use of atomic power, serves to reinforce the foregoing conclusions.

The prospect of atomic energy is usually discussed in the context of 'the nation's energy needs', where the measure of the nation's 'needs' is hardly more than an extrapolation of the existing upward trend in energy consumption. In fact, there are no *needs* in economics. The subject matter in economics turns on choices — individual or collective choices. And, clearly, collective choices made through the political process can alter the direction of any trend. A rise in electricity prices or in petrol taxes, a ban on automobile advertizing, increased subsidies to public transport, along with the creation of a social atmosphere in which (as in wartime Britain) manifestations of austerity are regarded as virtuous, could check and reverse the secular demand for energy. Such measures not only serve a policy of conservation for the future but, by reducing the current depletion rates of conventional energy supplies, they release resources and allow more time for research into technologies for making solar and tidal energy available at low cost.

Ecologists, conservationists and others concerned with the global spread of air pollution obviously prefer this solution of the so-called energy problem. Business and technocrats, on the other hand, impatient to maintain and increase the pace of economic growth, have argued for a rapid expansion in the production of atomic energy — for the time being through nuclear fission — in anticipation of making the economy increasingly independent of conventional energy sources, such as coal and oil, within the next few decades.

Although, as a result of public reaction to recent nuclear plant accidents, ambitious nuclear programmes have been pared down and delayed, such setbacks cannot be expected to reverse the trend towards nuclear power. In view of the continued pressures exerted by technocrats and businessmen, reinforced as they are by the clamorous demands of some Third World countries, an expansion in the world's nuclear energy capacity has to be anticipated.

Apart from the more familiar risk of failure of the emergency cooling systems (which function to avert disaster in the event of a reactor accident), the two main risks are associated with the production of poisons of two kinds: (1) the long-lived radioactive fission products, and (2) the production of plutonium, one of the deadliest elements ever handled by man.

The first risk (1) is connected with the disposal of radioactive wastes after their separation by a reprocessing plant. At present, the fission products which form a 'soup' of virulent radioactive acid that will be dangerous for hundreds of years tend to be stored in concrete-encased refrigerated stainless-steel tanks. The second risk (2) associated with the production of plutonium is yet more alarming. Bearing in mind that the half-life of plutonium is about 24,000 years — and that a mere half-

pound of it, dispersed into the atmosphere as fine in-
soluble particles, would suffice to afflict every living
mortal with lung cancer — the plutonium inventory that
accumulates over the years will constitute a carcinogenic
hazard for a thousand human generations.

A containment level as seemingly high as 99.99 per
cent would hardly be reassuring. Yet inasmuch as plutonium is a necessary material for the creation of nuclear
weapons, and is expected to be a highly lucrative item of
illicit traffic, such a containment level is unlikely to prove
feasible.

With such facts in mind, a recent statement by Dr
Hannes Alfven, a Nobel physicist, looks conservative.
Writing in the *Bulletin of Atomic Scientists* (May 1972) he
said:

Fission energy is safe only if a number of critical devices work as they
should, if a number of people in key positions follow all their in-
structions, if there is no sabotage, no hijacking of the transports, if no
reactor fuel processing plant or reprocessing plant or repository anywhere in the world is situated in a region of riots or guerilla activity,
and no revolution or war — even a 'conventional' one — takes place
in these regions. The enormous quantities of extremely dangerous
material must not get into the hands of ignorant people or desperados.
No Acts of God can be permitted.

To be more explicit, the extent of the vigilance required by the planned expansion of the nuclear energy
programme will entail an unprecedented extension of the
internal and international security systems. Among other
measures, this will involve armed protection of the transport network along which move containers of atomic
materials, a vast increase in internal surveillance and,
inevitably, the surrender to the police, or, possibly, to
specially trained forces, of extraordinary powers of entry,
arrest, detention and interrogation, if, as they will claim,
they are to move fast enough to prevent highly organized
criminals, psychopaths and fanatics from capturing positions from which they can effectively blackmail a nation
or cause, inadvertently or deliberately, irreparable
disaster.

THE PERMISSIVE SOCIETY

Let us now turn to a phenomenon that looks like the combustible product generated by high technology and affluence when combined with the commercial ethos — the so-called permissive society of the last quarter of a century. It is sometimes misleadingly regarded as an extension of 'the open society' or as a manifestation of a 'pluralist' society, whereas its significance is better appreciated by referring to it as the *amoral* society. Certainly, the term 'permissiveness' as currently used has no necessary affinity with the Western-type liberal democracy that is characterized by freedom of political debate and dissent. Instead, it is characterized by three interrelated developments: (1) more obviously, by a suspension of traditional norms of propriety and etiquette that is making the question of what is proper or improper, decent or indecent, especially with respect to sexual behaviour and to licentious entertainment and literature, increasingly a matter of individual taste and discretion, (2) by a decline in the respect for long-standing political procedures upon which all forms of self-governing societies have depended (occasionally expressed in open defiance of new legislation by interested segments of the public, or by attempts to obstruct its implementation through direct action or 'confrontation'); and (3) by the fragmenting of the moral consensus.

This last development is indeed portentous. For whatever our conflicts of interest, or our political differences about ideal or better arrangements for society, effective argument is stultified if there is no longer a common set of ultimate values or beliefs to which appeal can be made in the endeavour to persuade others. I doubt whether so fragile a social artifice as a liberal democratic society can continue to endure if each individual or, rather, if each of a small proportion of the individuals comprising a society, is to be his own ultimate authority in all that touches on propriety, legitimacy and morality.[19]

In fact, we are witnessing in our own times the dissolution of all such norms of propriety and civility that have held Western societies together. In particular, the spread of these self-styled emancipatory movements, whether agnostic or religious, racial or cultural, feminist or homosexual — along with a wanton proliferation of religious circuses, drop-out communities, witchcraft revival, Dionysian cults, guru-worshippers, fanatical millennialists, survivalists, neo-Luddites — all combine to undermine the framework of ecumenical faith, tradition and convention that holds together a continental and pluralist civilization.

On reflection, however, this permissive society may also be viewed as a providential development by means of which a technically sophisticated economy, under institutional compulsion to expand, may continue to do so in an already affluent society. For in these circumstances the continuous expansion of industry depends directly upon its success in whetting and enlarging the appetite of the consuming public as to enable it to engorge a burgeoning variety of new goods. A consuming public that looks as if it might eventually become satisfied with what it has, or a consuming public whose demand is restrained by traditional notions of good taste and propriety, or by firm ideas of what is right and wrong, will not serve. The required insatiability even in an age of reckless abundance can be ensured only by undermining traditional restraints, by subverting cultural norms and by encouraging promiscuity. In all the large cities of the West increasing numbers from all sections and classes of society, following the lead of neurotic artistes, sensation-seeking film-moguls, publishers, impresarios, and coteries of disorientated free-booting 'intellectuals', in their clamorous rejection of any limits to sensate experience — sometimes rationalized as joyous rejection of 'Victorian guilt' — are coming to believe that 'life enrichment' is to be attained simply by dedication to quasi-religious therapies and hedonistic pursuits.

Bear in mind that we are not talking of 'decadence' as commonly understood and often associated with an effete aristocracy or pseudo-sophisticated coteries. For modern industry to continue to expand, the decadence of a

minority would not suffice. Nothing less than the decadence of the consuming masses themselves is necessary.
And this spreading decadence of the masses — especially
thc younger masses — has in it little relish of refinement
or epicurism. Nurtured on the spicey pap of television
entertainment their tastes are becoming increasingly
vulgar and visceral, moving towards the sadistic. True,
many continue to go to church, but they act as if God is
not. If they turn for guidance at all, it is not to precepts
based on traditional cthics but to what they choose to call
an 'own ethic' — an ethic congenial to those in pursuit of
'autonomous self-fulfilment'. If they deign to justify their
conduct, whether inspired by impulse or calculation, it is
by reference to the strength and depth of their own
private convictions. The moral touchstone in effect has
become their 'absolute sincerity'. Alas, the appeal to
'sincerity' has always been the readiest excuse for in-
iquity. No historian can doubt the intensity of Hitler's
incandescent sincerity. And, as we know, Charles
Manson killed other men because he knew 'in his heart'
that he was right.

Convictions are one thing. Conscience is another. A
conscience is moulded within an ethical matrix — in this
context, an ethical matrix common to the great ecumenical religions. And it evolves through effort, through the
pain of repression, through fear, through love, through
example, through hope, beckoned by awakening aspirations to the good and, perhaps, by a need to feel worthy
of the grace of God. The individual conscience is not,
then, an autonomous creation. It is the manifestation of
man's spiritual heritage and, in settled conditions, forms
the core of the moral consensus by which a social order
survives.

I have stated elsewhere (*The Economic Growth
Debate*, 1977), as a judgment of fact, that a moral consensus that is to be enduring and effective is the product
only of a general acceptance in its divine origin. A moral
order, that is, can rest secure only on religious foundations. It cannot be raised on humanist principles, or on
enlightened sweet reason — at all events, not so long as

society continues in that corrupt state in which sinners outnumber saints, in which human weakness is more evident than human strength and in which temptations abound.[20]

The preceding sections of this essay argued that recent technological innovation in the West has created unprecedented ecological hazards and social conflict, and that the resulting rise in public apprehension has acted to invoke increased government intervention taking form as detailed legislation and an expansion of bureaucratic power. I am now suggesting that this trend towards larger government and, therefore, less personal freedom, is sure to be reinforced by the perils attendant upon our new permissive society. Not only does the popularity of the 'own ethic' concept undermine the traditional pride taken in personal rectitude, so threatening the efficient operation of industry and government; more importantly, it poses a threat of civility and order. In a society in which ideas of right and wrong become ephemeral and self-serving — in a society in which a growing number of people, single or in groups, feel free to act on their own privately reconstituted consciences; feel free to act illegally, and indeed criminally, for any 'worthy' cause — the resulting climate of unease, edginess and anxiety, along with the community's fear of anarchy, will eventually sanction surrender to the police, and to other internal security organizations, powers of surveillance and control that are incompatible with our present ideas of a libertarian society.

Thus as the moral order upon which any viable civilization has to be founded is eroded in the name of personal emancipation, so in the name of security must the state expand its powers. In effect, as repressive mechanisms internal to the individual are scrapped, repressive mechanisms external to him have to be forged. The permissive society, it may be inferred, is precursor to the totalitarian state.

IN DISMAL CONCLUSION

In sum, then, the growing threat to liberty arising from
adverse spillovers is the direct result of the direction
being taken by scientific and technological innovation.
Some innovations take the form of industrial processes
that generate a variety of dangerous pollutants; others of
new products that confer on the user a direct power to
cause harm or distress to others, especially in large urban
areas where people are inevitably in each other's way;
yet others will bestow on society such dreadful powers of
control as to induce in it a state of continuing anxiety.
The resulting demand for 'government regulation' and
'control' is reinforced by the spread of new hazards
produced by the very pace of modern research and the
haste to market its product.[21]

Whether the hazards created by new weapons systems
ought to be classified as spillovers is a question of
definition. What can hardly be doubted, however, is that
sustained research into yet more effective weapons of
offence and defence is itself an important example of the
broad thesis that the advance of science, though it
enhances man's power, also makes his world an increasingly dangerous place to live in. There is now so much
more that can go wrong. And the consequences of some
mishap or misdeed can be terrifying to contemplate.

Are there other considerations that might alleviate the
gloomy picture of the future depicted here? True, there
has been no attempt at comprehensiveness in this review
of recent developments. But I do not think that the
examples used to illustrate my thesis are altogether
singular or unrepresentative. Obviously, not all innovations create significant spillovers, and not all significant
spillovers act to augment government powers and to
reduce liberty. But many of those which are familiar to
us, and many which are confidently expected to occur, do
indeed appear to have these tendencies. And none I can
think of has strong countervailing tendencies.

Indeed, the more one reflects on the matter, the more
certain becomes the vision of the human race being borne

along by an irresistible tide towards an ocean deep-mined with unknown perils. As the perils loom closer, and as men come to apprehend their increasing vulnerability, the instinctive desire for self-preservation — found in organized societies as well as in individuals — will prompt them to cede to government far greater powers of surveillance, control and repression than are compatible with our contemporary notions of personal liberty.

NOTES

1. *The Sunday Times* (6 July 1975) reports the remarks of an American psychologist, Dr Thomas Narut, at a NATO conference held in Oslo, that convicted murderers were among those selected and trained for naval commando-type operations and also for serving as 'hit-men' in American embassies. Their training included the showing of films of violence designed to enable them to dissociate their feelings from the act of violence.

   Whether or not the report is true in substance, it is plausible enough and only one of many that occasionally come to the surface, create a stir, and then are forgotten.

2. The case is cogently argued in M. Friedman's *Capitalism and Freedom,* (University of Chicago Press) pp. 172 — 6.

3. A general account of the economist's approach to this phenomenon is given in my article 'The Spillover Enemy', *Encounter* (December 1969).

4. 'The New Inflation', *Encounter* (March 1974).

5. Contemporary inflation cannot be blamed largely on the steep rise in oil or food prices since 1973, as in all countries it preceded such movements.

6. Universal recourse to insurance schemes, even ideal ones, will not prevent this development since the premia will have to rise in proportion to the rise in medical expenses. State control of medicine, however, can take the profit out of using elaborate equipment and can otherwise regulate its use.

7. The moral dilemma of the physician at a time when traditional

values are in disarray is well described by Alasdair MacIntyre in 'How Virtues Become Vices', *Encounter* (July 1975).

8. The difficult moral and legal problems that would arise in the event of successful cloning techniques have been discussed by Leon Kass, 'Making Babies', *The Public Interest* (Winter 1972).

9. Apprehension is not confined to the general public. Modern medicine advances with extraordinary rapidity as a result of a variety of non-medical specialists, trained in chemistry, biology, mathematics, physics, engineering, biochemistry, and so on, all working on one or other narrow aspect of the subject, making their tentative findings available to the medical profession. But such is the profusion of new discoveries that the physician, especially if he is a general practitioner, has neither the time nor the training to form an independent judgment with respect to the new drug, new method of treatment or the new medical equipment in question. As is well known, many just read the leaflets sent to them by the drug companies and prescribe the drugs to their patients.

10. Government departments of food or health must expect to encounter difficulties in determining the risks of food additives. Among the reasons for recent difficulties that the US Food and Drug Administration (FDA) has in making decisions about food safety, Peter Hunt lists (1) the often-inadequate scientific-data base (he notes that the rapidly advancing scientific technology soon makes obsolete last year's level of detection of harmful substances), (2) the lack of agreement by scientists on the significance of the safety data available, and (3) the fact that there is 'no public or scientific consensus today on the risk or uncertainty acceptable to justify the marketing of any substance as a food or drug'. Admitting that subjective judgment necessarily plays a large role in safety decisions, the FDA has sought divergent viewpoints to help reach a consensus on particular issues. In this connexion, *see* Rita Campbell, *Food Safety Regulation* (Washington, DC, Ballinger Publishing Co., 1974), especially pp. 3 — 7.

    In order to meet these problems, which can only grow with time, the FDA has to expand its personnel, extend the scale of its operations and intervene more actively in the private sector of the economy.

11. It is far from improbable that there is a number of Thalidomide-type drugs widely in use having deleterious genetic effects that operate more slowly over time, making them difficult to detect. Indeed, *The Sunday Times* (25 May 1975) reported that each year about 100,000 women in Britain had taken pregnancy tests using

drugs that are currently suspected of giving rise to the birth of deformed children.

12. Around the turn of the century, German scientists working in the Bayer Company succeeded in synthesizing a crystallized compound from morphine, which was marketed under the trade name of Heroin. It was regarded as non-addictive, and it was recommended in medical journals as a means of treating morphine addiction. Ten years had to pass before heroin was recognized by the medical profession as highly addictive and dangerous.

Since the 1960s, methadone, a synthetic drug developed in the Second World War — also, incidentally, by German scientists — has been used as a substitute drug in the treatment of heroin addicts. After encouraging reports of success for many years, investigations undertaken by the US Drug Enforcement Administration revealed in 1974 that deaths from illicit methadone surpassed those from heroin, and that methadone constituted a substantial share of the illegal traffic in drugs.

A critical account of methadone's history is to be found in E.J. Epstein's paper, 'Methadone: The Forlorn Hope', *The Public Interest* (Summer 1974).

13. Food is the most complex part of the environment to which the individual is exposed. We are discovering that, in addition to nutrients, foods contain a large number of trace elements supplemented today by chemical additives, contaminants and other substances arising from the application of modern technology such as pesticides, animal drug residues and migrants from packaging. In recent years, the FDA has begun to adopt methods designed to incorporate risk-assessment into decisions for certain classes of food, and additional legislation may be anticipated.

14. The cumulative effect of fluorocarbons (from spray cans) and nitrogen oxide gases in dissipating the earth's protective ozone mantel would be one of such instances — except that few scientists today would dismiss the possibility as negligible.

15. 'Re-examining the Military Budget', *The Public Interest* (Winter 1974).

16. *See* the article by Mark Abrams, 'Changing Values', *Encounter* (October 1974), on recent social surveys in Britain.

17. A contingency anticipated by Roberto Vacca in *The Coming Dark Age* (1972).

18. Improved methods for identifying, tracing and incapacitating people are among the list of the 100 most likely innovations

compiled by Herman Kahn and Anthony Wiener in their book
The Year 2,000 (1972).

19. The growing amorality of the individual in a secular society as a
precondition to the fragmentation of its moral consensus is more
than plausible conjecture. Already there are also deep fissures
within Western societies dividing group from group. I am not
talking here of the dislocations caused by increasingly bitter
labour disputes. Among the 'white collar' classes in America,
there are already irreconcilable differences in philosophy and
belief as between, on the one hand, technologists and industrialists and, on the other, environmentalist and ecologists;
between, on the one hand, advocates of further liberalization of
sexual entertainment and display and, on the other, the so-called
moral majority, and a variety of fundamentalist and right-wing
organizations. Conflicts between them have more than once
erupted into violence. Nor patriotism, nor loyalty to common
ideals, nor common interests, nor a common enemy, can unite
them.

Another phenomenon needs mentioning in this connexion. The
current popularity of the 'survivalist' movement in America that is
making elaborate preparations to survive the believed-impending
nuclear holocaust. Billion-dollar survivalist industries have sprung
up selling everything from dried foodstuffs to sophisticated
weaponry. The hardcore survivalists are said today to number two
million, with about 17 million on the fringes of the movement.
They have formed communities in strategic geographical locations
all over the country, in part as a refuge from the nightmare of
crime that is taking over in some of the larger cities but in the
main to prepare themselves to continue to survive after the
holocaust — which is expected by some communities to occur this
year or the next.

Each of such communities hoards vast supplies of foodstuffs,
water, protective clothing, implements and machinery — enough
to survive a year or longer — and an arsenal of weapons in order
to defend itself against the hungry panic-stricken mobs that will
have escaped the nuclear destruction of the cities. With this vision
in mind, the men, women and girls of these communities undertake exhaustive guerilla-type training, ready to meet 'invasion'
with violence. Some of the communities are formed of religious
zealots and believe they are being directed by the word of God.
Many regard their government as corrupt and criminal, the
existence of socialism and communism as manifestations of
Antichrist, and the rampant homosexuality in the cities as the
miasma of social rot.

All the ingredients are here for chaotic internecine warfare —
whether or not the nuclear Armageddon occurs within the next
few years, as anticipated. Of the millions now acquiring lethal

weapons and expertise in the killing of potential attackers, some proportion may be tempted to make less laudable uses of their skills. Large numbers may become restless for action if Armageddon is delayed or the expected enemy does not turn up in time. Their intensive military preparations may find other outlets. Beginning with a fanatical determination to defend itself, a close-knit militant community, especially one guided by the word of the Lord, may move on to defend its principles, to attack the enemies of Christ and civilization, to purge the cities of evil...

20. There is, of course, no lack of instances in the records of history of religious corruption, religious fanaticism and religious persecution. Yet it should not be necessary to remark in such an essay that the value of religion to humanity cannot be dismissed merely because of the abuses to which it has frequently been put.

Perspective requires that a distinction be drawn between the inspiring spirit and purpose of an institution, and the improper uses to which it invariably lends itself; a distinction between the office and what it stands for, on the one hand, and on the other, the behaviour of the incumbent himself.

No man was more acutely aware of ecclesiastic intrigue, bigotry and corruption than was Lord Acton, the great Roman Catholic historian of liberty. But he ever kept in mind the distinction between the church authorities and the Authority of the Church.

As I remarked in my *Costs of Economic Growth* (Penguin, 1967), an institution disposing of the enormous wealth, power and patronage, of the Church, was a magnet for opportunism, attracting to its service men of worldly ambition. It is no cause for wonder that good men could be inflamed to battle under the banner of God when, in fact, the stakes were in the main temporal and material.

Who can say whether more crimes against humanity have been committed in the name of God (so breaking the Third Commandment), in the name of liberty, in the name of fraternity, in the name of justice — or in the name of any other virtuous attribute when it is tied to a slogan and brandished by a revolutionary movement inspired by an all-sweeping ideology!

For all the dark pages in the history of religion, I affirm my statement in the text that faith in a benevolent Deity is a necessary condition for the good life inasmuch as — for ordinary mortals at least — such a faith is the ultimate source of legitimacy for a society's morality and sense of right without which it loses its identity and cohesion.

21. Time is money, and it has become just too expensive to spend time uncovering the range of possible side effects of scientific innovations. On this point, however, Garrett Hardin writes:
The overwhelming probability is that any newly proposed remedy

won't work. More: experience shows that there is an almost equally high probability that the new nostrum will *cause* actual harm. The most intelligent way of dealing with the unknown is in terms of probability. Therefore we should assume that each remedy proposed will do positive harm, until the most exhaustive test and carefully examined logic indicate otherwise.

(Exploring New Ethics for Survival, W. H. Freeman & Co., 1972, p. 59)

7   The Future is Worse than it Was

OPTIMISTS AND PESSIMISTS

Let me begin with some gentle ridicule directed against those economists, technocrats and scientists who, in contemplating the future, err fatally on the optimist side, putting their faith in the evolving power of science and technology, and sometimes — incredibly — in the ultimate wisdom of men. Pessimists, such as I, come in for a deal of good-natured banter. Often enough I am accused of shouting wolf, of being a Jeremiah or a Cassandra; these accusations I never challenge. For the wolf in the fable eventually came. Jeremiah was a true prophet; as he foretold, so it came to pass. And Cassandra was invariably right, and because she was destined to be ignored, catastrophe befell the people.

Again, the optimists rejoice in reminding audiences that many instances of woeful tidings have been belied by history. True, but cheerful tidings have also gone the same way. I remind you that American President Hoover in 1931 assured his countrymen that prosperity was 'just around the corner' — it took nine years to turn that particular corner, and it would have taken longer had not war broken out in Europe in 1939. More than a century earlier in Britain, the chancellor of the exchequer Robinson foretold an era of unprecedented prosperity. After his announcement there followed an era of unprecedented depression, lasting until the 1840s. During this time the poor man suffered much embarrassment, being nick-named 'Prosperity Robinson' by the public. In a desperate attempt to escape ridicule (if I may add a footnote to this episode) he managed to get himself elevated to the peerage as Lord Goderich. Alas, the public promptly switched to calling him 'Goody Goderich'.

And, while on this subject, let us recall that a little earlier, on the eve of the French Revolution, the mood of all progressive elements in Europe concurred with Wordsworth's ecstatic exclamation: 'Bliss was it in that dawn to be alive, but to be young was very heaven!' Soon after, Madame Guillotine was working overtime, Paris became a shambles, Robespierre perished in the terror he had organized, and for two decades more, in the name of liberation, the armies of Napoleon looted, pillaged and spread carnage throughout Europe.

On the other hand, I admit that more than once, especially before the eighteenth century, the end of the world was prophesized — though for reasons, incidentally, that would be regarded as far less rational than a similar forecast of calamity today. But there is little comfort to be had from the optimists' unnecessary observation that it didn't happen. It has only to happen once!

In parentheses, and surrendering to an honest impulse, I ought to add that in assuming the mantle of a doom-sayer I am 'batting on a strong wicket'. The public does not readily forgive a man for arousing joyful expectations that are subsequently foiled by events. But if my gloomy prognosis turns out to be wrong, nobody, I am sure, will bear me a grudge. At any rate, fortified by this reflection, I shall journey with firmer tread through the shadow of the valley of death.

THE SIMPLE-SIMON ECONOMIST

But at the outset, I am obliged to make a short digression. I have to address myself to those persistent and consoling messages that emanate from the type of economist I shall unkindly refer to as Simple Simon. Simple Simon has about him the quiet strut of the confident hard-nosed realist. He keeps his eyes on the figures, on the economic data; and, indeed, on little else. I do not exaggerate when I say that Simple Simon bids us ignore current estimates of the global reserves of scarce resources, and to look instead at the record of economic developments, and especially at the recent trend of prices. Accepting conventional methods of estimation, the 'real' prices[1] of nearly all the important raw materials have been declining over the last century. They have continued to do so — though less markedly — over the last ten or twenty years. From this glance at the figures we are expected to deduce that there is a strong presumption that the decline in these prices will continue in consequence of man's resourcefulness and innovation. *Ergo,* we are not to worry; we may continue to ransack the earth's limited resources with impunity. It may be that, at some time in the future, prices of raw materials will sound a warning knell, and if so, the market will come into its own, using the higher prices to ration the scarce resources.

The argument invites comparison with the method of determining whether Vesuvius will erupt by taking the temperature of the soil in a strategic cave half way up the volcano. Simple Simon, we may imagine, trudges up there once a week every Saturday, and each time he returns to the citizens of Pompeii with the reasuring news that, if anything, the temperature of the soil is falling.

One dark day, a Wednesday, flame and smoke belch from the crater. The earth shudders and groans, and lava is seen bubbling around the crater rim. Simple Simon rushes up the mountain, reads his thermometer, and returns in triumph to the citizens of the now-doomed city of Pompeii to confirm that the temperature of the soil is now indeed at record height. He has proved to them that his instrument is an infallible indicator.

I am saying that it is something like this which can, today, so easily happen. Bearing in mind that the world's consumption of many important raw materials is doubling over relatively short periods — short periods varying from ten to thirty years — we shall one day notice that prices are shooting up, and that they show no sign of levelling off. Like that infallible thermometer, however, prices can tell us only that the worst is happening: they can do nothing to remedy the situation. We may be faced with an acute global shortage, possibly an irreversible one. Should crops fail badly in two or three successive years, through soil exhaustion, through some baffling disease or from the ravages of a new unconquerable pest (the mutant product of decades of chemical pesticides), famine and plague could rack the world's population. Even the optimists among us would agree that such a prospect is not inconceivable and, if they were honest, that it is also far from being implausible.

Simple Simon, however, continues to argue that since environmentalists cannot offer satisfactory evidence of an impending shortage, while the economic record has been, and still is, that of falling prices, the world's economies should continue their efforts to expand without restraint.

But the responsible citizen will demur at this conclusion. Unless we have good economic reasons (based on expected changes in relevant magnitudes) to believe that price trends *will* continue, the existence of a trend tells us virtually nothing about the level, or the direction, of future prices — as so many stock-market speculators have sadly discovered.

What is at issue, in such circumstances, is the methodological one about the burden of proof.

Let us, therefore, forego the satisfaction of presenting evidence that would go some way to dispelling complacency about future resources. Let us suppose that we do not know whether or not usable resources, plus technological progress, will suffice to allow the modern economy to continue growing for an indefinite period. Let us, if you like, suppose that prices of raw materials are declining and, for the foreseeable future — in this context for the next two or three years — will continue to decline; how does a prudent decision-maker act?

Consider the two alternatives. If governments and industry heeded the alarmist views of the environmentalists, and events proved they were wrong, the consequence could hardly be called painful. We should come to realize, after the event, that we consumed less voraciously than we might have done — and, therefore, we have left for the future more capital than we need have done.

If, instead, governments and industry were guided in their policies by Simple Simon's conclusions, and events proved that Simple Simon was wrong, the consequences could be extremely painful and possibly disastrous. Technology might be quite unable to cope in so short a period with a simultaneous shortage of a large number of important raw materials, with soil erosion, with seemingly indestructible pests or with a critical level of poisons accumulated in the biosphere from the spread of new chemicals and synthetics. The consequence, that is, could be global and irreversible disaster.

To take such a chance, even if the chance were small, would be more than folly; it would be the betrayal of a trust, a trust assumed by each generation to leave to the generation yet unborn not only the heritage of a once-beautiful earth — this perhaps is no longer possible — but to leave them at least the means of survival. And yet, under the institutional compulsion of the modern economy, government and industry and citizen are, indeed, taking just such a chance, electing to play dice with the lives of future generations.

A GENERAL THESIS

As prolegomenon, a statement of simple fact: Any year now, any day, any moment, some lunatic, some fanatic some desperado, is going to give the signal, turn the handle, push the button, pull the lever ... and the holocaust will have started, with a good chance of exterminating life on earth. The chances of our civilization surviving the end of this century are small. On any sober assessment of the peril in which we stand, we should have to concede the point. Yet, since we somehow contrive to disbelieve it, it is necessary to be emphatic.

The peril in which we stand is wholly without precedent, even when considered by reference to biological time. To compare the present with the dangers that threatened earlier civilizations would be false to history, false to sensibility, false to proportion.

Over the last 6,000 years, civilizations have risen and fallen; fallen from internal corruption or external conquest. Christendom in the West has more than once come close to extinction, almost overwhelmed by the warrior hordes led by Atilla the Hun in the fifth century, and again in the eighth when the sword of Islam was at the throat of Europe. Less than half a century ago, Europe lay prostrate under the heel of new barbarism. Over those 6,000 years, the world has, from time to time, been ravaged by plagues, by pestilence and by famines.

But never, ever, by a threat so imminent, so grisly, so ghastly, so absolute, as the one we face today. Once the so-called balance of terror is upset — and in truth its equilibrium is unstable (and will become more so as additional countries, often led by fanatics, come to possess the means of nuclear destruction over the next two or three years) — millions, hundreds of millions, of people, may perish within minutes. All the higher forms of life can be destroyed or irreversibly damaged. After hostilities the planet may be covered with radioactive dust and ash from which life, as it has evolved over millions of years, may never rise again.

I interject these remarks early, in order to unsettle you a little; because, for a short time, we have to unblur the imagination in order to think dispassionately, if we can, about the unthinkable — as if we were intelligent beings on a distant planet gazing with incredulity through some prodigious telescope at the behaviour of *homo sapiens* on the small planet earth.

But observation alone is of limited value unless we have already formed some broad explanatory thesis enabling us to interpret all the endless scurrying about that we observe through the telescope. So let me present you with a general thesis.

I speak with imperfect recollection of the details of a true story (told by an American physician) about a man who, having a spot of arthritis in his finger joints, was given some tablets by his doctor as a result of which he developed a stomach ulcer. The doctor operated on the ulcer and injected the patient with strong antibiotics which so interferred with his cardio-vascular system that the doctor felt obliged to perform a number of minor operations. The patient became weaker and was referred to a heart specialist. In his weakened condition he contracted a lung infection and, nothwithstanding the continual attention of three doctors and the intensive care of the hospital staff, expired within two weeks of the heart operation. As it transpired, then, after the high-powered medical treatment had all but destroyed the patient, the doctors using more high-powered medicine, prolonged his life for those two weeks.

This case, I am assured, is not atypical. But no indictment of the methods of modern medicine is to be developed here. I have bigger fish to fry. For the true story you have just heard is illustrative of modern technology, taken as a whole, for which the ordinary man is the victim. Western civilization today is in the position of our hapless patient during his final two weeks. If there were a withdrawal of modern technology — if, for example, there were a universal breakdown of the electricity supply our civilization would probably not survive above a few weeks. At the same time, the course of technological progress looks destined to destroy us, and should we, inexplicably, survive, looks to destroy any hope of the good life.

Just as the medical treatment to which our patient was subjected wrecked his natural system and rendered him wholly dependent from day-to-day upon artificial means of sustenance, so does modern technology act to destroy the natural systems of human organization which embody institutions that generate cohesion, stability and resiliency. In more immediate terms, any current technology which is designed to meet a problem, real or imagined, is more likely than not to create new problems, as a result of which new technologies and new institutions come into being which directly or indirectly produce further problems, and so on.

These new problems arise not so much from economic growth as conceived and measured by economists but from scientific and technological progress itself which continues irrespective of the movements of GNP and related indices. I have argued in earlier works that such progress has exacted a heavy toll in terms of human fulfilment,[2] especially since the Second World War, and I believe that this toll is likely to become heavier in the immediate future; indeed, that the danger of rupturing the fabric of our civilization is real and imminent.

THE FUTILITY OF OUR ECONOMIC OBJECTIVES

Economists might be willing to concede that the existence of consumer freedom of choice with respect to market goods, along with freedom of choice of occupation and enterprise, though undoubtedly good in themselves, provide no assurances for the quality of life; that, indeed, such rightly coveted economic freedoms are quite compatible with a decline in the quality of life. Thus, when the evaluating economist says that he will equate an increase in social welfare with an increase in the area of (market) choice for individuals, he is — or he should be — aware of the weight being borne by the *ceteris paribus* clause.

It is not merely the fact, which many economists now realize, that there can well be *too much* choice — an incredible array of new brands and models and designs that bewilders more than it delights the consumer. Far more significant is the implied requirement of constancy of the individual's tastes and of his capacity for enjoyment. In reality both are certain to vary over time in the modern economy, and indeed to vary rapidly with the continuing changes in the material conditions of life. Inasmuch as production technologies and the goods they spawn alter radically within a person's lifetime, the urban environment — the size, architecture and atmosphere of the cities; the unending swirl of traffic, the incessant clamour, the assault on the senses — along with an entire style of living also alter rapidly and, in doing so, alter for better or worse the behaviour, attributes, belief systems and communal aspirations. These changes are the vital factors that ultimately determine the welfare of the members of society, yet they do not lend themselves easily, if at all, to measurement on a scale of better and worse.

Thus any serious endeavour to understand the operation of the economic universe must begin with a recognition that the all-too-familiar indices of economic changes, and trends amount to near-irrelevant abstraction. They constitute, in fact, an economic-numbers veil that, over time, serves to conceal a shattering succession of urban transmogrifications, social upheavals and spiritual crises, that are the unavoidable by-products and, therefore, the critical reality of modern economic activity.

Nonetheless, the far-reaching social transformation that has occurred since the turn of the century can be pondered, interpreted and debated intelligently if not perceptively. To be sure, an informal reflective approach to any set of phenomena, physical or social, elicits condescension if not contempt from the quantitatively orientated specialist obsessed with the statistics of hypothesis-testing. Such attitudes, however, are unwarranted and ill-founded. A serious student comes far closer to an understanding of the way Americans actually lived in the 1820s from an acute observer such as de Tocqueville than from any conceivable pile of econometric studies directed to estimating real income, distribution or trade imbalances.

At all events, my critique of the conventional economic world-view of recent history is developed in terms of observation and interpretation, with only incidental regard to magnitudes. From a number of interrelated themes associated with the material progress made in the West since the turn of the century, I shall restrict myself here to two: first, the futility of the chief social objectives commonly accepted and currently pursued by governments everywhere irrespective of political complexion and, second, a conjectural assessment of the human consequences of the so-called microcomputer revolution. The gist of the writings of the more articulate growthmen reflect a persistent belief — a belief which has become official doctrine for members of the 'Enlightened Establishment' — that a continuation of those developments most closely connected with economic growth must culminate in a better life for the citizen. These developments, the measures of which are then used as indicators of social welfare, include (1) more and better goods, (2) more income equality, (3) more education, (4) more mobility, and — although there are now dissenting voices — (5) an extension of the social services. My brief comments on each of these popular social goals are intended to suggest that, if more time were available to us, a respectable case could be made for the contrary view; that continuing endeavours to realize each one of them is more likely, on balance, to reduce human welfare than to augment it.

MORE IS WORSE

(1) Since so much has already been written, pro and con, about the value of more and better goods in the post-industrial world, I shall confine my remarks to little more than a summary of my more sceptical reflections.

In conditions of destitution or hard poverty no reasonable man will dispute the importance of more consumer goods; in particular, more food and shelter. I remind you, therefore, that we are *not* considering the plight of populations in the less developed countries but the plight of populations who live in the countries of the West or, more generally, in the so-called affluent or post-industrial societies — and live in material conditions to which the poorer countries aspire as a matter of course.

In these affluent societies the bulk of the working population — according to recent surveys — regard themselves as middle-class. And of the dwindling minority of the 'proletariat', or manual workers or 'blue-collar workers', the larger proportion enjoy earnings which compare favourably with the better paid clerical or 'white-collar workers'. In a physical sense — and certainly as compared with the material conditions prevailing in the third world countries — there are goods a'plenty for the mass of the people. Even among the poorest 10 per cent of the population, which can legitimately claim to be suffering from 'relative deprivation' — there are few who suffer hunger or real physical hardship.

In the post-industrial society the first and most significant characteristic to emphasize is its self-defeating ethos. For in order to ensure the absorption of increasing amounts and kinds of the products and services of modern industry it has been found necessary to devote considerable resources to the creation of want-dissatisfaction — effectively to inflame the spirit of dissatisfaction with one's existing possessions, with one's style of living, with one's status, with one's accomplishments and education. The intent and effect of media reports and comments, of official attitudes and establishment propaganda, and of course of the omni-present commercial advertizing industry, are directed continually to renewing the springs of discontent in economic man — which is hardly a prescription for promoting human fulfilment. Indeed, it represents a notorious perversion of the putative ends of economic endeavour, as repeatedly stated by economists, which is to use material resources to produce 'want satisfaction'.

It is hardly surprising then that many of the goods produced and consumed have their rationale reversed; rather than being perceived as ends they are perceived as means, or also as means; rather than regarding goods as goods in themselves they have become psychologically transmuted in greater or lesser degree to indices of success in life.

Economists in the West have, of course, long been aware of this characteristic propensity of their somewhat over-motivated citizens to regard the main purpose of life as that of 'keeping up with the Joneses'. In economist's slang this propensity is referred as the 'Jones' effect' and is formalized in the statement that the welfare of the citizen depends, *inter alia,* upon his command over market goods *relative* to those of others.

The implications of the undeniable existence of this Jones' effect is a thorn in the side of the pro-growth lobby. For the more this Jones' effect predominates — and it is destined to grow in affluent societies — the more futile is the policy of raising per capita consumption as a means of increasing the general welfare.

Again, a mass consumption economy in the affluent society, being one of continuing innovation and there-fore, also, of rapid goods-obsolescence, necessarily breeds a throw-away attitude towards man-made goods irrespective of their use or performance. There is no time to grow fond of any possession no matter how well it serves. For it will, in any case, soon be superseded by a new brand or model. In time, almost everything bought, including 'consumer durables', come to be regarded as potential garbage and therefore treated as such.

Moreover, a mass-consumption economy that emerges from a mass-production economy rests heavily on stan-dardization. The 'Age of Abundance', it transpires, is abundant with pre-packaged and chemically processed foodstuffs, with plastic knick-knacks, with plug-in machines and fine-tuned equipment. A part of the price that people in the West pay for this unending procession of shiny assembly-line products is the concomitant loss of those now-rarer things that once imparted zest to people's lives — the loss of individuality, uniqueness and flavour; the loss of true craftsmanship, of local variety and richness; the loss of intimacy and atmosphere, of eccentricity and character.

Again, and thinking primarily of continuing innovation in the provision of products and services, a further develop-ment should be borne in mind. A large proportion of the consumer innovations that have appeared since the end of the First World War is of the kind that acts to distance us from our fellows. Thus the by now all-too-familiar auto-mobile, the radio, the stereo, the television and, of course, the increasingly popular home-computer are also the ele-gant instruments of our growing mutual estrangement.

These are the kind of innovation that have multiplied over the last few decades, perhaps being 'labour-saving', inevitably so. Today we can shop in the supermarket without speaking a single word to any one. In business also, in banking, insurance and in travel, the ratio of personnel to customers continues to decline year by year. Increasingly we are identified by code numbers and express our wants by filling in forms and pushing buttons. The greater part of the clerical staffs in a wide range of agencies and businesses spend the working day pressing keys and gazing at the flickering green letters which race across miniature screens.

And this withdrawal from direct communication with others has much further to go. Technically speaking, the greater part of education at all levels can be done by television on open or closed circuit and by computer teaching machines. Although we are loathe to recognise it, teaching personnel could today be radically reduced, and the greater part of school and university buildings made obsolete. Those international conferences, beloved of businessmen, civil servants and academics, are on the verge of being technically unnecessary since satellite television link-ups have been developed.

Physicians are learning to depend upon the computer for diagnoses, and visits to the local doctor or medical centre will decline as people learn to respond to computer-screen questionnaires about the nature of their symptoms. In hospitals, patient-monitoring devices make the bedside attention of nurses unnecessary — the temperature, pulse rate, blood pressure, and so on, of each of several score bed-patients can be read on a central panel by a single nurse who will direct attention to a particular bed only when a critical reading is registered.

Again, games like chess and bridge can now be played by a single person matching his skill against the computer.

One could go on listing instances of innovation that have come into being, or are coming into being, which in the ordinary commerce of life removes us from direct contact and intercourse with our fellow men. Since the turn of the century, then, and with increasing rapidity, we have come to depend both for our needs and for our entertainment upon the products of technology and ever less upon the physical presence, upon the direct help and company of other human beings. In consequence, the direct flow of feeling and sympathy, so essential to the sense of being and living, becomes increasingly blocked as channels for their expression fall into desuetude.

To add an important footnote, these innovations that keep us to ourselves, that keep us indoors and in our automobiles, also keep people off the streets and so act to encourage street crime. The nuclear family — which, of course, better serves the modern economy's need for a highly mobile workforce — is also a family that is unlikely to strike roots. The individual can no longer count upon the moral support and the sympathy of an extended family group, or upon a neighbourhood or community in which he is known, a community within which he and his parents and perhaps also his grandparents were reared. As the American author Vance Packard observes in his *Nation of Strangers* (1972), the chances today in America, at least in the larger cities, are that a family does not know the names even of its immediate neighbours.

Since the foot-loose city-dweller has no commitment, then, to the vicinity in which he is currently residing, and since he is unable to depend upon the support and the loyalty of members of a community, it is not surprising that he does not wish 'to become involved', to use a popular American phrase. If he sees a crime committed before his eyes, he is as likely as not to turn the other way. He may hesitate even to inform the police lest he, or a member of his family, be victimized. In this way, and in other ways to be mentioned presently, the unprecedented rise in street crime and violence in Western countries over the last thirty years can be traced back to technological innovation.

As a final observation we may turn to a theme developed by the Scandinavian economist, Stefan Linde, in his *Harried Leisure Class* (1970), a theme that might be expressed in a re-coined phrase: too many goods chasing too little time.

Families in the West, especially in the USA, are already under strain from the weight of abundance. Quite apart from inroads into their pattern of living made by the demands of their automobiles and their television and video sets, they are beset by the problem of time; time that is necessary to use their assorted sports gear and other recreational toys, time that is necessary to avail themselves of travel opportunities and 'new and exciting' forms of entertainment.

Alas, they are finding that, there being only twenty-four hours in a day, it is time itself that places an irremovable constraint on their powers of consumption. Already, all too many of them live in a state of animated frustration amid the growing opportunities for accumulating possessions, and for recreation, entertainment and travel. Their homes are littered with newspapers, reports and magazines that are scarcely glanced at, with books that never get read, with old transister clocks, with electric gadgetry that is hardly used, with bargain clothes seldom worn, with discarded sports equipment, with drawers full of gifts, impulse-bought gew-gaws and bric-a-brac — and on tables and desks and shelves, piles of subscription forms, postcards, sales catalogues, travel brochures and jottings and memoranda.

How unsurprising then is the common complaint that 'there is never time to do anything'. Each day is felt to be incomplete; scarcely begun before it is over. One wonders nostalgically about an innocent age of man long ago when, as in childhood, time was abundant, when the hours lingered, the mind wandered, and the senses opened to the joys of the here and now.

EQUITY, EDUCATION AND MOBILITY

(2) Turning to the belief that continuing economic growth is necessary for a more equitable distribution of incomes, one is bound to be sceptical. Despite extensive

and determined government intervention, economic growth over the last three decades has not succeeded in making a significant impression on the distribution of 'real' disposable income. Nor would I care much if it did. While I would not deny the case for more discriminating methods of removing the remnants of hard-core poverty within the wealthier nations, the case in welfare and justice for spreading purchasing power more evenly among their citizens is dubious. Elaborating new techniques for the measurement of what we now call 'relative deprivation' will continue to provide occupational therapy for some economists. But in those countries where the overwhelming majority of families live far above subsistence levels, it is not a concept that can excite genuine compassion. Current preoccupation with distributional issues in the West springs in the main from a growing impatience and envy among competing groups in a society whose economic life is shaped and powered by an ethos productive of restlessness and discontent. Certainly, the goal of material egalitarianism, as a component of social justice, has no panoramic appeal — even if it could be realized without political coercion. If it has a philosophical vindication, it is one that rests on the belief in a deterministic universe, one in which each individual is wholly a victim of circumstances he is powerless to influence.

(3) The goal of increasing higher education serves the needs of economic or rather technological growth itself since so much of it is vocational and technical. This sort of higher education is not education in the classical sense. It is not education in the humanities. It has no direct affinity with art or culture or civilized living. Indeed, the liberally educated man is today a figment. A man may be literate and well-read in a popular book-review sense. But he can be 'educated' only over a minute strip of the expanding spectrum of knowledge.

Hence the universities, or 'multiversities', the centres today of what cynics call 'the knowledge industry' are, in the nature of things, no longer able to produce educated men, or men of cultivated intelligence. They are geared to produce specialists, in particular scientists and technicians. The hyper-refined specialization involved in post-graduate work, which cramps the spirit and warps judgment, is the antithesis of the older ideas of education.

Even the spirit of humanity, and toleration, wont to be associated with the university, seems to have evaporated. Developments since the Second World War have made it evident that, in its new populist version, the university can no longer be thought of as a sort of secular cathedral conducive to detached reflection and uninhibited conjecture and debate. It is fast becoming a microcosm of the larger community. Into it are imported not only the political passions and prejudices of the community at large but also its fashionable aberrations and trendy 'liberation' movements. It is sad to recall, moreover, that on so many occasions over the last decade, the one place within the Western democracies where a controversial issue could *not* be publicly debated were the university precincts.

Seen in perspective, the surrender of the original ideas of the university as to conform with a high-technology mass-consumption society, with its emphasis on vocational training, may be associated with the decline in the status and the influence of a more leisured and educated middle class and, consequently, with the decline of what used to be called the social graces, a decline in urbanity, a decline even in civility.

(4) Let us turn now to the goal of increased freedom of movement, long linked with the idea of progress, sometimes in the naive belief that travel broadens the mind. Whether in fact the package-tour explosion of the postwar era has done much more for the affluent masses than to narrow down the number of places worth travelling to, is doubtful.

The private automobile has multiplied like the locust, and like the locust has swarmed over and eaten the heart out of our cities and resorts. We think today of the ambient environment, whether urban or suburban, largely in terms of traffic opportunities or problems. We live, eat, work, sleep, in the midst of it all. Times and distances, road conditions, highway routes, peak hours, short cuts, traffic lights, freeways, one-way streets, road signs, parking spaces, auto repairs, car prices, car accidents, auto accessories, fuel bills — all these, along with the perpetual din, the dirt, fume and danger, have become the everyday preoccupation of our hurried lives. New car-towers identify the modern city which since the Second World War has become more of a venue for arrivals and departures, a place of perpetual transit and repair, one more node in the country's intricate network of roads and freeways, junctions and airways.

There are, indeed, many things essential to the good life that the market cannot be expected to produce. Of itself it cannot bring into being, nor can it ensure the existence of, the boisterous gaiety and the intermingling of animated crowds strolling along boulevards and about city centres. The operation of the market cannot ensure that the city is built on a human scale; for people not for cars; for the hum of human voices not for the interminable roar of traffic. The operation of the market cannot of itself bring dignity, harmony or inspiration into the urban environment.

Neither can the institution of any system of property rights help (even if property rights were distributed equitably among the populace, they would be sold at the highest market price to motoring interests and ambitious developers). The great cities of antiquity (Athens, Rome, Antioch, Babylon), the cities of the early Renaissance (the statued squares and palaces of Florence and Venice) and the Georgian crescents of London, all these were not the products of a commercial spirit. To be sure, wealth was needed, but it was not enough. This ennobling architecture arose from the ethos of a particular civilization, to be sure a more élite civilization than our own, one in which wealth and culture, life and art, were more close interknit. Possibly, only in smaller communities set in a less frantic age than ours can the current of civic pride flow strong and steady, and provide both the impulse and the dedication to create from stone and marble and glass and space a physical environment of grace and harmony, a source of joy to the citizen and an expression of faith in his future.

THE NEED FOR THE COMPASSIONATE STATE

(5) Let us turn finally to those incurably optimistic liberals credulous enough to discover in the rise of the welfare state the emergence of what they love to call 'the compassionate society'. Reference instead to the 'compassionate state' would provide a more revealing terminology.

In order to appreciate the origin and the *raison d'être* of the 'compassionate state' one need not go far back in history: in Britain, to the collapse of the self-sufficient village community in the wake of the agricultural revolution, in the latter part of the eighteenth century, followed by the so-called Industrial Revolution. A century later, particularly after the Second World War, urban and suburban communities began to fold up. For in an increasingly mobile and anonymous society — each family equipped with its own set of electric labour-saving gadgetry, its television screen, its stereophonic equipments, its private automobile — people have become too hurried, too stretched, too strained, too 'motivated' and too fearful of 'slipping behind' or 'missing out', to find the time to know or care much about their immediate neighbours. Indeed, over the last two decades, the media have reported innumerable instances of people being victimized in public — that is, of being visibly assaulted, robbed, raped and even murdered — while passers-by and lookers-on refuse to get 'involved', not even bothering to call the police.

At all events it is just because, in our new super-affluent super-mobile mass civilization, ordinary people have begun to live under conditions in which they are evidently unwilling or unable to help or to care for each other that the state has, perforce, to expand the umbrella of its welfare and rescue services. In effect, since direct interpersonal compassion can no longer be depended upon in the new rootless metropolitan society that modern technology has brought into being, compassion itself has had to be *institutionalized;* it has therefore, in this form had to be administered, in part by large voluntary organizations but, in the main, by an army of state employees. Not surprisingly, however, this army of state-employed social workers come to have a strong vested interest in their vocation. As with all state bureaucracies, the members seek to augment their power; in this instance by seeking ways and means of increasing the numbers of their 'clients', and the range of services that the government provides.

It is important to understand, moreover, that the growth of this 'institutionalized compassion' not only replaces the personal compassion of the more traditional community, it also facilitates and fosters the spirit of irresponsibility — irresponsibility which is an important component of the psychological underpinning of the so-called permissive society. Just as a person has the choice of adopting regular health habits which require self-discipline or, alternatively, of indulging himself in all that strikes his fancy (in expectation that his abused body can be repaired when necessary by the medical profession), so society makes a similar choice — and clearly has made a choice. As a whole it has chosen to be a 'reactive' rather than a responsible society. It has chosen to indulge itself in all innovations showing commercial promise, undeterred by evidence of the cumulative damage both upon the physical environment and upon the health and the character of the citizen. After all, a hideous environment, a population increasingly prone to nervous diseases, a rising trend of family breakdown, disorientated adolescents, youth delinquency, a phenomenal increase in pregnant schoolgirls, and so on — all these untoward developments offer vast opportunities for social workers, supports their cry for more funds, for more social workers, for more counselling centres, for more psychiatric clinics, and for more scientific research!

THE COMPUTER UTOPIA

I turn, finally, to consideration of a development that is sure, incidentally, to increase the size and the power of governments, the microcomputer revolution. As I indicated at the beginning of my talk, mention the possible dangers of a new development and the knee-jerk reaction of our dedicated growth-men is to make merry with the clangour of false alarms that have run along the corridors of history. A global shortage of vital resources? What rot! Did not so eminent an economist as Jevons make a fool of himself by forecasting a shortage of coal before the end of the nineteenth century! Have not English writers since the time of Chaucer been lamenting the disappearance of the English countryside? Consequently, if I speak of this coming micro-electronic transformation of industry, and the fearful problems we shall struggle to cope with, you may depend upon it that complacent colleagues will at once hark back to the forebodings voiced during the 'Industrial Revolution' and will be eager to remind me that it brought prosperity to the world and immeasurably improved the material condition for the working man. *Ergo,* we are not to worry. (Nonetheless, I might add in a footnote that a large proportion of two generations of working-class Englishmen suffered untold misery, and that 'the dark satanic mills' of Lancashire were a terribly reality to numberless women and children who were brutalized, deformed and went to an early grave. There were also frequent revolts, and more than once in the first half of the nineteenth century, England was near the edge of civil war.)

We may aptly refer to this dark episode of history as an earlier transitional period since I am addressing myself to this new industrial revolution which has just begun. Yet the difference between this new industrial revolution and the old is as remarkable as, in the military sphere, is the difference between gunpowder and atomic missiles — a difference of destructive power so great as to constitute a difference in kind.

And we are not talking of the future; the future has

already arrived. Already it is technically feasible to use micro-electronic control devices as to render superfluous, in government, industry and commerce, the greater part of the existing workforce.

The jobs that are becoming economically unnecessary are not only those that are monotonous, exhausting, distasteful or dangerous. Computer design systems can perform faster and more accurately the skills of the ploughman, the printer and the designer. Microcomputers are replacing typists in offices. Developments in telecommunications, and in the storage and manipulation of information, now threaten the functions of middle management and personnel. Computers that amass the accumulated knowledge of leading experts in the field will take over the greater part of the work of professional administrators, lawyers, doctors, and others. As indicated earlier, patient-monitoring devices in hospitals will drastically reduce nursing staff. Personnel in travel agencies, in banks, in government offices, are being replaced by sophisticated machinery. Shopping in supermarkets will become superfluous as home links with terminal computers (possibly making use of the telephone system) take over. Industrial robots, once used for restricted operations, such as paint-spraying and welding, are now being designed to run machine tools and to do general assembly work, including such intricate jobs as installing lights in car instrument-panels. I have read of a company in Japan making robots which manage automated machine tools, and which can run five different machines at once.[3]

General progress in the design of computers of increased versatility and capacity is today so rapid that it has to be dated in months, not years. The transformation of the post-industrial economy has already begun, and one may confidently anticipate unprecedented labour turmoil over the next two decades. Only the tunnel-visioned technocratic mind can ignore the terrifying problems that will face modern nations during an indeterminate 'transitional' period, and prematurely rejoice in the prospect of wealth and leisure to be placed within the grasp of all.

Conventional economic nostrums will have very limited application to a situation when, within a few short years, millions of workers in all the industrial countries will find their hard-earned skills superseded by micro-electronic devices. Let us look briefly at the alternative ways of coping.

(A) Attempts to maintain high employment with comparable hours of work is hardly feasible for two reasons. First, since any manual or mental skill that can be reduced to a routine or to a response-system can be taken over by a micro-computer, it is more than just possible that the kind of work at present seemingly beyond computer capacity (the work that in a computer economy still remains to be done by humans) — innovative activity, and work on computer designing and repairing — may also be beyond the capacity of most ordinary men and women. The larger part of a modern nation's potential labour force will, for the first time in history, be literally unemployable. Secondly, even if by some miracle the whole of such labour force could be productively employed, it would create output levels of products and services that are likely to exceed even the alleged insatiability of the American citizen, who, as alleged earlier, can no longer find the time to enjoy the uses of his accumulating possessions and the growing opportunities of amusement.

B. The other alternative is obviously increased leisure for the masses — a capital idea, an age-old dream to be realized at long last! But consider the difficulties. First, just how much education, culture and recreation can the ordinary person imbibe? How much more travel is possible? Cities, beaches, resorts the world over are barely able to accommodate the existing numbers of tourists. How much home television-computer entertainment can an unemployed adult stomach each day before wanting to scream? Second, what of the psychological strain of having to live with the knowledge that one is permanently unemployable. In all hitherto-existing society, a man's daily work has been his anchor holding him to the real world, a ballast steadying his life, a routine imparting structure to it. If today so many older men, with dwindling strength and energy, become distressed or demoralized when compelled to retire from productive activity, how much harder will it be for the young and energetic to adapt to a life of compulsory leisure? To the man receiving it, a profit, a salary or wage is more than just a pecuniary return to his enterprise and effort: his remuneration is also perceived as a form of recognition, an assurance that the community places a value on his services however humble. The payment for the services he renders is thus also a source of a man's self-esteem without which he is a pitiable creature.

Of course, our dedicated growth-men are sworn never to see problems; only to see 'challenges'. But recourse to semantics cannot assure their being met satisfactorily. Some problems may indeed be well 'beyond the wit of man' to resolve. Those mentioned above appear to me to fall into that category. We may confidently anticipate labour troubles galore over the next decade or so.

Beyond that, unlimited leisure for the mass of people looks to me to be a necessary economic consequence of the microcomputer revolution taking place in the prosperous countries of the world. But if such a mass-leisure society can be made viable, official propagation of a new concept of the purposes of life would be necessary, reinforced by new institutions and by more embracing forms of state control. For in a society of human drones, the risk of anomie or demoralization, and the reactions to it in outbreaks of hooliganism, rampage and revolt would be intensified. Already, it seems the best we can hope for is a society akin to Aldous Huxley's *Brave New World*.

To conclude, I have been unable, alas, to conform to the popular convention that bids the speaker end on a high note, or at least a note of hope. I do not believe that there is any escape from the dilemma facing us: if we are able to survive the perils posed by ecological hazards, by the permissive society and by the incipient computer revolution, it can only be at the cost of a more embracing

and more repressive state. For so grim a prophesy, I beg
your indulgence.

NOTES

1. The price of the raw materials relative to the wage index (and
    even to the current price index).

2. In *The Costs of Economic Growth* (Penguin, 1967); *The Economic
    Growth Debate* (Allen and Unwin, 1977).

3. As is well known, Japan has (May 1982) more robots than the rest
    of the world put together. In two or three years it is expected that
    robots will machine and assemble other robots. It has been
    estimated that by the year 2000 there will be 10 million robots in
    Japan — nearly 10 per cent of the current Japanese human
    population.

8 Religion, Capitalism and Technology

PROLOGUE

The Current State of Religious Faith in the West

Although there exists today a greater variety of religious denominations than ever before, the view that there has been a continuous decline in religious faith in the West, at least since the Enlightenment of the second half of the eighteenth century, is common enough. The post-war proliferation especially in North America of new movements, denominations, orders, factions and cults, both domestic and imported, is best interpreted as a manifestation of religious faith in the throes of disintegration.

True, some religious organizations have never been strong on faith. While it continued to be a pillar of the Establishment from the Restoration of 1660 onwards, the Church of England grew in the regard of the public more as a peculiarly British institution than a branch of ecumenical Christendom — rather like the game of cricket, in which any show of passion would be deemed unseemly.

A cynic might well say that to ask a Church of England cleric what his beliefs are would be considered bad form. A sporting interest in the contents of the Bible might reasonably be expected of a vicar. But one could hardly aspire to the mitre without having also established a reputation as a liberal agnostic.

If Trollope's novels are any guide, this doctrinal urbanity is not a recent development. The younger sons of county squires would customarily have to make a choice as between entering the legal profession, embarking on a military career or taking holy orders, weighing up the net social advantages with the help of friends and relations.[1]

With the possible exception, in the Barsetshire novels, of
the curate Mr Crawley, all of Trollope's prelates, from
the most humble prebendary to the bishop — agreeable
men for the most part, though often eccentric — were
invariably quite busy with the things of this world and
conscious always of the importance of a good domestic
and social life in spreading the influence of the Anglican
Church.

The Modern Church of England
Today, the Church of England clergy has progressed only
in enjoying life less and in involving itself more with
man's welfare here on earth than with his immortal soul.
The institution has, indeed, begun to look very much like
an extension of the social services of the modern state.
Many a local church, like the YMCA, offers amenities to
the young and practical advice to unwed mothers and
Borstal boys. Your average Church divine prides himself
on being a practical man. He is not likely to be caught off
guard thumbing his Bible. More often than not, his
breezy affability conveys the impression that he has a far
livelier interest in the affairs of this world than of the
next and, moreover, that there is very little about this
wicked modern world that he is not comfortably familiar
with. Church of England sermons, over BBC radio, begin
to sound each year more like editorials from *Modern
Living* magazine — although, in deference to tradition,
served up with a light sacramental garnishing.

Lest I be accused of exaggerating the cultivated worldliness of the servants of the Anglican Church, let me
remind you that Bishop Robinson's 'Honest to God'
monograph gently chided those gullible churchgoers who,
as he put it, pictured God as 'an old man in the sky' or —
not to put too fine a point on it — as a personal God
rather than a pantheistic force. His worldliness was
further manifested in a *Sunday Times* article (1969) in
which he welcomed the permissive society and the
pleasures it afforded of gazing at nude bodies — while
covering his flanks from attack by men of smaller vision
by contriving a distinction between erotica (good) and

pornography (bad).[2] With examples such as this to draw
upon, it is not surprising that churchmen, increasingly
concerned to 'do good' here on earth — and at a time
when economic and political judgments are increasingly
difficult to make — are losing influence and respect.

The nadir was reached (or was it?) when the World
Council of Churches found itself making financial contributions to South African terrorists — invariably represented by that newspeak term 'liberation fighter'. In
newspaper articles and letters (in the British press) its
spokesman sought to vindicate such action by *realpolitik*
considerations, among which was included the argument
that the ends (liberation from the yoke of white rule)
justify the means (the use of bullets and bombs to maim
and murder innocent people).

If we exclude a dwindling minority of true believers to
be found more often among the older generation, members of the Anglican Church are unlikely to find in their
religion any impediment to their worldly ambitions.
Indeed, it can well serve to extend them. On both sides
of the Atlantic, although more so in North America, the
considerations that enter into the choice of a particular
church or chapel bears comparison with those that enter
into the choice of social club. And it may be more
important to a business or professional man to belong to
a Masonic lodge or to a Rotary club than to a Church.

By far the greater proportion of the Roman Catholic
Church is no less worldly, although it is a good deal more
superstitious. Generally, Catholics are dimly but uneasily
aware that the Holy See is fighting a rearguard action for
survival against the sweep of world fashion (the ordi-
nation of women priests), against global imperatives
(reducing the growth of world population) and, more
particularly, against the more recent findings of secular
disciplines and the immense and increasing prestige of
science. In the meantime, the mass of Catholics prefer to
confess their sins than to curb them, to hedge their bets
by offering incense to a variety of saints, acting as if an
all-knowing God is yet too foolish or too busy to remark
their blatant hypocrisies.

The Religious 'Resurgence'?
Turning now to the so-called resurgence of religion, or
rather religions, in the post-war period, more counterfeit
than current is to be found in it. Much that looks at first
glance like reversion to an older tradition, such as the
'moral majority' movement in the USA, is best understood as, in large part, a recoil from the excesses of post-
war 'permissiveness', which permissiveness itself is both a
response to historically unprecedented mass affluence
and a reaction to the psychic stress of modern living.
Much like the earlier movement for Prohibition in
America, which gathered its strength from Puritan elements and the more conservative small towns, it cannot
prevail against the psychological drive and institutional
innovations impelled by modern economic growth.

New fundamentalist movements, like the older
Jehovah's Witnesses, appeal to those who want 'to come
out of the cold', to struggle out of the spiritual void that
is the legacy of the Scientific Enlightenment. Fundamen-
talism in varying degrees is characteristic also of an
assortment of evangelical movements of mixed provenance. Watching the faces of soul-starved audiences trans-
fixed by the pugnacious rhetoric of Bible-thumping
ranters of the Billy Swagger variety — reminiscent of
Sinclair Lewis' Elmer Gantry — one is momentarily
reminded of the faces of concentration-camp inmates at
the sight of food they despaired of ever tasting.

In all age-groups we shall find those who seek wistfully
for signs and for wonders, turning in their anxiety to
astrology, to pagan rites or to Oriental gurus. Others
there are — denizens of Jacque Ellul's *Technological
Society* — who conceive of religion as offering techniques
for achieving tranquility (TM) or for releasing 'potential'.
Scientology, blending ancient myth with modern superstition, offers its initiates a *scientific* religion putatively
designed to enable them to cope successfully with the
body and pressure of the times. Yet others, taking their
cue from the more wanton features of post-war permissiveness, seek to found Dionysian cults, or to transform
aspects of Christianity into pop or freak religions, or

jazzy ones, like the 'swinging Jesus' movement, or else to
seek thrills and perhaps secret power in pursuit of the
occult, in witchcraft or in Satan-worship.

From Christendom to Religious 'Pluralism'

One might want to continue sorting out, identifying and
interpreting the variety of shrill noises emanating from
this post-war Babel of 'irrationalist' recidivism. But such
a fascinating exercise is best reserved for another occasion. Instead, as historians, let us mark the stages in
the spiritual journey made from the ecumenical Christendom of the Middle Ages, through Reformation and
Counter-Reformation in the Western World, down to
what we might euphemistically call the religious 'pluralism'
of the last quarter of the twentieth century. Is it possible
so to deceive oneself as to associate this phenomenon
with a revival or resurgence of religious faith — approv-
ing of it with cynical detachment as offering to the individual 'an increase in the area of choice', to use the
economist's jargon? Does it really amount to more than a
medley of frantic cries lost in a spiritual tundra? Certainly very little of this post-war religious renaissance has
struck root and taken blossom in the Western world in
the form of a resurgence of rectitude and virtuous conduct, the essential products of a serene faith and trust in
the Divine.

Far removed we are today from the religious climate of
the early Middle Ages. Over all the hardships, cruelties
and other deficiencies of that time, a sacramental religion
suffused life, lending to even the ordinary events of the
week, the season, the year, a dignity and transcendental
purpose. In an age such as ours, abounding with technical
vitality, all the events in an ordinary person's life shrink
into insignificance. Religious organizations have need,
themselves, to employ technical innovations in order to
be heard above the ignoble clamour, and even the more
respectable denominations of Christian and Jewish religions are not above borrowing the resources of science
and salesmanship in bids to attract a wider membership;
not above veering with the winds of political fashion —

twisting doctrine a little in response to feminist and other
liberation movements — not above revamping ritual,
litany, scriptural interpretation, as better to accommodate the tastes and style of the modern disorientated
mind.

In sum, if a sceptical interpretation of the recent
course of religious activity in the West is accepted, it will
be seen as evidence not of a growth in religious faith but
of a decline — the anguish of religion in its death throes.
Explanations of this impending collapse are not hard to
come by. My own explanation, possibly very imperfect
and (if plausible) possibly not altogether novel, follows.

INTRODUCTION

The Modern Anomie

De Grazia's *Political Community* argues cogently that in
any society ordinary men have a deep-seated need for
leadership and authority. It is painful for them to live
without firm beliefs, beliefs not only in their origins or
their destiny or in their institutions, but beliefs also in
persons, in heroes, in myths, in gods. And, I may add,
the pain of unbelief can be aggravated by other factors
inseparable from a high technology civilization; in particular, by a welter of innovations that have incidentally
produced a style of living that is responsible for the
anomie peculiar to the modern age. The elements comprising this anomie include mutual estrangement in urban
areas, family disintegration, growing apprehension of the
hazards of new technologies, a sense of loss of control —
attributes I shall touch upon later.

But whether this anomie or despair — that which
technocrats scorn as 'loss of nerve' — has in fact been
active in moving the Church, some Churches, towards
socialism (as vaguely comprehended) is an auxiliary
question, one of secondary importance and, in any case,
one that cannot be answered with any great confidence.

Unless one has some particular Church or faction of a
Church in mind, the belief that there is a movement of

ecclesiastic opinion favouring socialism, at least when understood as collectivist economic planning, is far from evident. Fundamentalist religions certainly have no truck with that kind of socialism. It is circumspect to place the word 'socialism' in quotation marks since like so many ideological terms — liberty, equality, fascism, democracy, anarchy, imperialism — it is encumbered by a weight of emotive associations and means very different things to different people.

What Does 'Socialism' Entail?
At one end of the spectrum we may identify the term with what Lionel Trilling called the 'adversary culture' of a bourgeois society, a phenomenon recently illustrated and deplored by Irving Kristol *(Encounter,* 1980). If all that is meant by 'socialism' is this sort of antagonism to, and distrust of, 'the system', and of the mass culture and commercial ethos it produces, it has been all too common a reaction since the Second World War, and indeed is familiar to the social historian as a reaction to contemporary life that can be traced back to the beginning of the nineteenth century. If Christian Churches, and Christians themselves, are believed to be moving towards 'socialism' in this sense, then it is an unremarkable tendency, one shared in some degree by the greater part of modern societies, although more especially by the 'educated classes' to be found in academia, in the professions and in many departments of government.

If at the other extreme, however, we use the term in its more precise economic meaning, as a form of social organization in which the 'instruments of production' are collectively owned and are directed by the state to fulfil a succession of economic plans, then, as indicated above, the proposition that the Church, or the Churches of the Western world, have been moving towards 'socialism' is doubtful.

I might add, as a gratuitous footnote, however, that even if it were a true proposition, it could easily be explained. After all, those who are repelled by the unrepressed manifestations of corruption and social injustice in the 'bourgeois' or 'capitalist' society in which they are immersed are sorely tempted to repose their hopes for social justice, for personal dignity, for human fulfilment, in that as-yet unrealized ideal socialist dispensation that will spring up joyously, after the successful revolution, from the ashes of the older order. Yet it is a temptation that cannot easily withstand sustained reflection. For even a casual romp through the pages of modern history would be enough to convince an open-minded thinker that the wanton enthusiasm that sweeps a revolution to its crest is soon transformed into alarm and dismay as 'enemies of the people' are discovered by the legion, as the blood-letting begins, as the struggle for power culminates in an unprecedented tyranny — and as veteran idealists in the West bewail once more 'a revolution betrayed'. At any rate, having left behind me the reckless revolutionary fervour of my early youth, and advanced towards the outskirts of maturity, I am content to endorse the epitomized judgment of Dr Johnson that 'the remedies for the ills of society are palliative, not radical'.

In the circumstances, I shall not dwell upon the evidence of the existing antagonism to 'bourgeois culture' in the West, or upon the disillusion with so many aspects of our post-industrial civilization. These widespread attitudes have been chronicled by many historians and sociologists. Instead, I shall argue that such a development is all but inevitable in a technically dynamic society. I shall further argue that such antagonism and disillusion are themselves linked to the decline in religious faith, and that the religious decline is itself an unavoidable consequence of the secularization of thought and feeling in a civilization shaped and controlled by the expanding powers of a Scientific Establishment for which, seemingly, no achievement is impossible.

To endure, a civilization requires a certain moral consensus. For a person like myself who believes that any such moral consensus has to be grounded upon religious foundations — upon an acceptance of the great myths from which humanity in all ages has drawn its spiritual

sustenance — the prospect before us is not only surpassingly sad, it is also surpassingly grim. For it follows, as I
indicate later, that the chance of our Western-type civilization holding together much longer in the absence of a
wide extension in the coercive powers of the state is
negligible.

CAPITALISM AND FREEDOM

Why the Malaise?
To represent the adversary culture today (as does Kristol)
as a form of ideological rejection by the intellectual and
middle classes of the values of a 'bourgeois' society is to
underrate the strength and sweep of the current of discontent that courses through our society. Intellectuals or
would-be intellectuals are, of course, more vociferous
than others, more articulate in their protest and more
habituated to attributing causes and, occasionally, to
proposing solutions. But the dissatisfaction with the
overall dimensions — the style, pace, pressure, artifice —
of modern living takes many forms and, in different ways
and different degrees, affects the greater part of all
Western communities. I begin, therefore, by putting the
rhetorical question: why, despite the exultant claims of
technocrats, despite the excitement of political events,
despite the pervasive sales euphoria and the unprecedented popularity among the masses of the get-away
package tour, is there so persistent a sense of malaise? Is
it just possible that people have begun to detect beneath
the shiny synthetic skin of our affluent civilization something that feels like a malign growth?

Allowing this impression to be true, the explanations I
offer for it have little direct connection with capitalism
or, more generally, with the institution of private property, private enterprise and the operation of free markets.
It seems proper, therefore, before attempting to explain
the prevailing discontent and the adversary culture it
produces, to prepare the way by indicating briefly the
position I take in the eternal debate about the relative

economic and political merits of market (or 'mixed') economies on the one hand, and of socialist (or collectivist) economies on the other.

Socialism vs the Market: A Preparatory Classification

I confess at the start that I have a strong predilection for the latter. I am persuaded of both the historical and logical connections between capitalism and freedom, both political and personal — a theme propounded over the years by writers in a variety of disciplines, and more recently argued with lucidity and conviction in the more popular works of two distinguished Nobel Prize-winning economists, Friedrich Hayek and Milton Friedman. I am in no doubt that the extending power of the state, even in the most democratic country, diminishes choice and weakens the power of the individual *vis-à-vis* the bureaucracy, enmeshes him further in detailed legislation that, incidentally, endangers the rule of law. The growth of the state's 'citizen protecting' functions, especially its mass welfare services, entails tax rates that encourages tax evasion and so, also, contempt for the law, at the same time as it acts to undermine the independence and character of individuals, many of whom become adept at 'milking' the welfare services as a way of life. To boot, the modern state undertakes enterprises that can be more efficiently performed by private industry. It introduces a welter of regulations that almost invariably strengthens the monopoly practices of the industries putatively being regulated. Worse, in the attempt to gain electoral support, big government has become economically so powerful that today members of new ethnic groups, as well as highly organized industries, repose their hopes for material advance more on the prospect of government economic aid or privileges than on individual effort and enterprise.

Indeed, government beyond a certain size and economic power will convert libertarian democracy into populist democracy. They offer prizes to everybody. The executive power appeals in the main directly to the electorate, making ample use of the media, keeps its eye

on public opinion polls and surrenders to the temptation
to bend principle in order to maintain popularity. It talks
perpetually of 'the national interest' while appraising
almost every measure in the light of its effect on the next
election.

No one more than I would welcome a contraction of
government to a fraction of its current size. Yet I am
certain that however cogent are the reasons for constricting and contracting modern governments, they will
expand in size and power over the foreseeable future.[3]

Why The Adversary Culture?
Returning to the need to explain the popularity of the
adversary culture mentioned above, I shall first consider
some of the features of the operation of existing economic systems, both market (or 'mixed' capitalist) and
collectivist, that may be thought vulnerable to criticism,
and attempt also to assess their importance. I shall then
move on to those factors, associated with technological
progress, which I hold to be crucial to any understanding
of the spirit or, rather, the dispiritedness of the times.

In ascending order of importance — and perhaps also
in descending order of detachment — the subjects I
discuss will be grouped under three headings:

(1) Some inadequacies of economic systems with
respect to consumer or producer bias, stability, choice
and risk.

(2) The failure of economic systems to cope with
spillovers, with some emphasis on post-war hazards
resulting from the pace of innovation.

(3) Broader connections between technological progress and the quality of life.

I end the essay with reflections on the basic incom-
patibility of science and religion, and on the incidental
inhumanity of science.

INADEQUACIES OF EXISTING ECONOMIC SYSTEMS

A Preliminary: Some Familiar 'Inadequacies'

Unemployment and inflation are topics that are too controversial to be broached in this essay. They are less disturbing and not nearly so unnerving as are the other phenomena we shall discuss in the last two sections. During the inter-war period, unemployment was undoubtedly one of the considerations, if not the chief consideration, that disposed people in the West to favour the ideal of socialism and economic planning. Since the war, however, increasing disenchantment with Soviet-type utopias, and widespread scepticism about their economic and social claims, have reconciled populations in the West to being more tolerant of their own economic ills. Moreover, the experience in the West of near-full employment for about thirty years after the Second World War has left the impression that unemployment is not, as Marxists would have it, an inevitable feature of a capitalist system. It is regarded, rather, as a 'recession' through which we are passing in a bid to reduce inflation rates to more tolerable levels. There is concern, but not despair.

Again, I shall say very little here about fears of an impending shortage of natural resources; no more than to voice my opinion that the reasons some economists give for their optimism are ill-founded: the classic (Hotelling) optimal depletion path is vulnerable (the discount rate in an inter-generational context does not, in any case, meet the conventional economic criterion); a quite unwarranted confidence is placed on the price trends of raw materials over the last fifty or a hundred years, and, in general, there are too many 'ifs' and 'buts' lurking behind the facade of confidence.

As for the current concern at the continuing global destruction of vast ecological reservoirs and of areas of natural beauty, or at the rapid extinction over the past thirty years of species of flora or fauna, it is one that I share. And I can conceive no system of enforceable property rights that would effectively reverse these world trends. I am resigned to the near certainty that should humanity survive that long, my great grandchildren will come to inherit a world of dwindling wild life and few accessible retreats of unsullied natural beauty. Theirs will be a more desolate, uniform and monotonous planet. For this dismal consummation I do not blame the market but the growth both of technology and population that, as argued by Richard Wilkinson in his *Poverty and Progress* (1974), are mutually reinforcing.

Environmental problems are as bad or worse in existing Soviet economies. More benign forms of socialism are, of course, readily conceivable (as are more benign forms of capitalism). But they are not emerging. Environmental concern is certainly not high on the list of priorities for the kind of socialist state as envisaged, say, by the British Labour Party's Tony Benn.

Consumer vs Producer Orientation in the Market

Turning to the consumer bias of the market, I have no criticism of those instances in which workers are attracted to moving into new areas of industries by the prospect of material gain or net advantage. The more troublesome case, however, is that in which, following a shift of consumer expenditure, capital and labour are subject to the 'discipline of the market'; in this connection one thinks in particular of workers who are laid off by declining industries and who, in addition to enduring anxiety and perhaps some hardship until re-employed, are impelled to incur search costs and, later on, possibly moving costs, retraining costs and also those 'psychic costs' associated with leaving a familiar neighbourhood and settling the family in a new one.

To devise some quantitative criterion that would compare an increase in consumer satisfaction from maintaining his freedom of choice in respect of market goods with the consequent increase in hardship suffered by workers is not an easy task for the economist. Even if it could be demonstrated that in almost all important cases the losses suffered by members of the community in

their capacity of workers or resource-owners exceeded
the gains conferred on members of that community in
their capacity as consumers, economists could always fall
back on the long-term advantages of having a more
flexible and dynamic economy. Without drawing any firm
conclusions, however, it is reasonable to conjecture that,
as the vicissitudes of consumer demand grow in the
affluent economy, the entailed trade-off of consumer
satisfaction for worker dissatisfaction, resulting from the
unchecked operation of competitive markets, becomes
less beneficial: in high consumption societies, increments
to existing consumer choice become less valuable whereas 'increments' of worker readjustment become more
irksome.

Technical Advance and Individual Uncertainty
Expectations of increasing versatility of consumer
demand arise chiefly from technical advance. In the first
place, the mass affluence in Western countries produced
by technical progress leaves a greater margin for 'impulse
buying' in contrast to those countries where the bulk of
consumption expenditure is restricted to staple items
(even the demand for luxury items by the wealthy in such
countries is relatively stable). This 'fickleness' of consumer demand, especially within broad categories of
goods, is aggravated by competitive advertizing and by
international competition. Looked at *ex post*, then, the
value to society of consumer freedom under prevailing
conditions in the West is easy to overestimate.

In the second place, and associated with the decline in
freight costs over the last hundred years or so, the
greater part of the goods currently being traded between
industrial countries are close substitutes for one another,
thereby conferring only limited benefit — as compared,
say, with the benefits from international trade between
countries producing goods that are complementary to
each other's economy. The fierce international competition today in autos, stereos, television sets, cameras,
watches, computers, cassettes and a host of other modern
devices and accessories, if allowed to prevail without

hindrance, could be vastly disruptive of the domestic economy and could inflict anxieties and hardships out of all proportion to any sober estimate of the consumer gain to be derived from the often bewildering assortment of hardware in the stores. The tariff and trade controls despised of economists are, of course, the means by which producers and workers seek to protect themselves from loss and hardship.

In the third place, continuing innovation entails not only new goods but new technologies, the adoption of which can overnight make hard-earned skills virtually obsolete. In these circumstances it is easy to understand the obstinate resistance of workers to the introduction of more efficient technologies, and also to understand the growing concern of labour unions not merely with real wages but with maintaining the actual employment level of their members and ensuring large compensatory sums in the event of dismissals arising from 'reorganizations'. If such trends continue — and there is no reason to believe otherwise — the problem will become more acute since market mechanisms of themselves can do little to resolve it. Through its political decisions, then, society as a whole may be seen as being more willing to sacrifice some consumer choice in order to reduce the strain on domestic producers and workers. Irrespective of union action, international trade and domestic industry are likely to be subject to more government control, not less.

State controlled economies, such as those within the Soviet bloc, are not so wealthy as those of the West, and the scope for 'impulse buying' is therefore correspondingly smaller. But even were they as wealthy, consumer demand would almost certainly not be allowed to disturb the detailed pattern of industrial production planned for the period. Job security therefore might well be greater.

To sum up, the consequences of the consumer bias of competitive markets in conditions of affluence and rapid technical change — in particular, apprehension among workers of their skills becoming obsolete, and of their becoming technologically unemployable — are among

the secular problems that I believe will grow in importance. But they are not, just now, among the most vital.

FAILURE OF ECONOMIC SYSTEMS TO COPE WITH SPILLOVERS

Pollution and Disamenity
We turn next, in this section, to the growing attention
paid in Western countries to the many forms of pollution
and disamenity that are subsumed under the umbrella
term 'spillover effects', those incidental effects and products of legitimate economic activity. Over the past two
decades the economic literature on this topic has swollen
to astonishing dimensions, a significant part of the resulting controversies being of a doctrinal nature. At one
extreme, within orthodox economics, there is the Chicago
School holding to the belief that with more carefully
delineated systems of property rights the unfettered
market can cope comfortably with spillover problems. At
the other extreme perhaps are those economists who, like
myself, are churlish enough to dismiss this belief as a
doctrinal delusion: indeed, to maintain that, given any
realistic extension of property rights, the contribution
that can be made by markets, no matter how flexible and
competitive, to resolving the allocative problems presented by the sort of spillovers being generated in the
present state of technology is miniscule. I give reasons
for this pessimistic view in the following section. In the
present section I wish only to remind readers of one
aspect of the spillover problem; an aspect, incidentally,
that is implied by the title of the recent popular book
written by Professor and Mrs Friedman, *Free to Choose*.

As the Friedmans convincingly argue and illustrate, the
more the public sector takes over from the private sector
of the economy, the less the choice remaining for the
individual: his money is used by the government to
produce goods he may have no interest in consuming or
in amounts he may not wish for. But expansion of
government in displacing private enterprise is not the

only phenomenon that effectively reduces individual
choice. As I argue in my essay 'The Effects of Externalities on Individual Choice' (Ch. 3 of this volume), the
expansion of the incidence of spillovers is another source
of choice-reduction, one that is certainly no less potent.
For irrespective of the allocative efficacy of property
rights — irrespective, that is, of whether the operation of
the market in any particular instance is able or not to
generate an optimal level of pollution as commonly
conceived — individual choice necessarily declines as the
extent and variety of spillovers expand.

Pollution and Freedom of Choice
If the keen environmentalist deplores the increase in
smog or the increase in aircraft noise within his vicinity,
it affords him no consolation to be assured by the economist that, bearing in mind transactions costs, and so on,
the disamenities he deplores are being produced at
optimal levels. He may himself have no use for the goods
produced by the smog-creating activity or for air travel
services. And even if he did have some use for them, he
still has no choice but to bear with the incidence of
disamenities being generated. He cannot, so to speak,
decompose these packages of goods-*cum*-bads (any more
than can the recipient of government largesse); he cannot, that is, at market prices choose *both* the amounts of
the market goods in question — autos, industrial products, air services — at market prices, and *also* the
amounts of the 'bads' he is willing to absorb. Under these
conditions he is worse off than he would be with a tied
sale, since he can always refuse the tied-sale package if
on balance it will make him worse off. He cannot, in
contrast, refuse the market-goods-*cum*-environmental-
bads package, no matter how much it offends him. He
has no choice but to bear with the environmental bads —
or strive to reduce them in some degree by incurring
costs — as and when they appear.
    Thus in an area of great sensitivity having occasionally
far-reaching effects on society's welfare, the operation of
competitive markets — even where property rights are

such as to issue in optimal outputs — can offer no protection to the individual. If it is believed that spill-overs as a whole will grow over the future, then whatever gains may be made from the exercise of individual choice arising from a hoped for expansion of the private sector of the economy, and from the production of new goods, will have to be offset by losses of individual choice in respect of environmental goods. And there can be no certainty that the balance will be favourable.

I need hardly add that I do not see a centrally planned economy, in the same stage of development, dealing any more successfully with the problem.

Technology and the Nightmare Prospect
Difficulties of dealing satisfactorily with environmental spillovers extend to a new dimension once we move from the familiar instances of smoke, noise, effluent and mutual interference that are popular in the conventional economic model, towards a veritable epidemic of new spillovers that have descended upon the globe since the Second World War — fears about which are a part of the incipient nightmare about the future that has come to blight the American dream.

These new spillovers spring chiefly from two sorts of technologies that carry a risk of local or global disasters. The first involve the spread of virtually invisible indus-trial wastes that if allowed to accumulate beyond critical levels could destroy man's habitat, or destroy man him-self. The second arise from the manufacture and use of new synthetics, chemicals, food additives, drugs, fertil-izers and pesticides, the long-term health and ecological effects about which, singly or in combination, we as yet know precious little.

The almost daily discovery of new hazards,[4] and the media publicity accorded them, has begun to effect a fundamental change in people's attitude towards science and technology. They have begun to see themselves not only as beneficiaries of technological progress but also as its victims. Public alarm and the consequent opposition to certain technologies have occasionally thwarted the plans of governments and planning agencies who, in their turn, believe that the safety assurances being demanded by vociferous segments of the public threaten the nation's economic future. As indicated in my essay, 'Road to Repression' (Ch. 6 of this volume), such developments are acting to increase state power and, therefore, to diminish individual freedom.

TECHNOLOGICAL PROGRESS AND THE QUALITY OF LIFE

Some Preliminary Classification

Turning to the all-important connections between modern technology and the experience of living (other than the effects mentioned in the preceding sections), let me concede at the outset an adherence to the following propositions in order to avoid unnecessary and often trivial controversy:

(1) That acting within his budget and within existing legal constraints, a person choosing among *market* goods, old and new, places a value on them that reflects his anticipation of benefit. Indeed, economists such as I, employing evaluative techniques, seek to estimate anticipated benefits of communities of individuals at different points of time — *not* their subsequent or *ex post* assessments.

(2) That the progress of science and technology over the last two centuries has made available to ordinary people living in the richer countries of the world a range of goods producing comforts, conveniences, experiences and entertainment that could not even be imagined by earlier generations.

(3) That there have been many instances of scientific discoveries and technical innovations that have conferred seemingly unambiguous benefits on society, and that there may well be others potentially able to do so.

(4) That modern medicine and hygiene has reduced infant mortality, contributed to the prolongation of expected life, and eased physical suffering.

In return for these handsome concessions, growth-minded economists who also recognize the notion of optimality might concede the *possibility* at least that the optimal level of technology — optimal with respect to human well-being — was reached at an earlier period in Western civilization than the last half of the twentieth century. So much by way of civil interchange and ground-clearing before giving utterance to scepticism.

The Need For Moral Criteria
From glancing through the pages of a large number of erotic and sex magazines, available along with numberless manuals on sexual techniques, displayed on the shelves and in the windows of ordinary bookshops in large cities (also in the campus bookshop of many a North American university), one discovers that many pages are devoted to advertizing vibrators and other electric gadgetry for women. The impression that a majority of American women over sixteen today possess one or more of these obliging instruments is borne out by private inquiries. Here, indeed, is a prime example of an expansion in the area of choice, which the orthodox economist must unquestioningly translate into an increase in social welfare, that has taken place within a decade or so. Over the same period, the bounty of technology has also provided us with an astonishing range of chemical poisons and quite a cornucopia of offensive-defensive small weaponry, from silent submachine rifles to letter bombs, from spring-blades to mace sprays.

These outlandish examples are chosen to persuade us that even with due regard to the *ceteris paribus* clause, an expansion of consumer choice may not always conform with our notions of an increase in welfare. Granted this much, we can open up with a weightier generalization: within a social order premised on insatiability, where, perforce, the tenth commandment is more honoured in the breach, and where it may be cynically affirmed that life has become a progress from discontent to discontent, any assessment of the value of the goods that people come to choose, and therefore the sort of life they come to lead, has to be referred to other than economic criteria. If the currents of modern life are to be judged by reference to criteria of taste and propriety, to artistic and cultural criteria, to religious and moral criteria, we must be prepared for discouraging conclusions. If we are concerned, again, with such attributes as social felicity and cohesion, or with the integrity and character of individuals, we must be prepared to be saddened by the course of events. If we wonder seriously whether the post-war period has witnessed a growth in serenity of spirit; whether there has been a growth in courtesy, tolerance, mutual trust; whether there has been an improvement in family life — we are impelled to answer in the negative.

With the advantages of hindsight one may conclude that these and other untoward developments are not really so surprising. Indeed, I hope to convince some of you that worse is yet in store. Yet to earlier economists, reformers, humanists and historians who wrote during the eighteenth and nineteenth centuries, such developments would appear not merely as aberrant but as monstrous. Macaulay, the great Whig historian of the first half of the nineteenth century, the apostle of progress, representing the spirit of mid-Victorian England in all its brash overconfidence and certain that material progress would be followed by cultural and moral progress, would be horrified at the tasteless vulgarity of modern life and appalled at the eruption of urban violence that disfigures the 'post-industrial' society of the West. For he shared with John Stuart Mill and others the belief that the growth and diffusion of wealth would act both to elevate taste and enhance morality. Among the later Victorians, we may pick out Matthew Arnold as one among many who agitated for the spread of education in the serene belief that in the fullness of time, and with the growth in the nation's prosperity, the cultural treasures of the world would be available to all classes, affording 'sweetness and light' and edification to ordinary men.

The Culture of Modern Society

Alas for those far-off innocent days. Matthew Arnold has been spared a visit to the modern mega-university where young philistines stalk the campus, pocket computers at the ready, where the bulk of the student body come to have their plastic minds pounded into a shape necessary to cope with the electronic machinery of a high-technology economy. In these sprawling knowledge-factories humming with technical equipment, where the young seem to have lost the art of linguistic expression, the traditional notion of the university as a community of scholars and the notion of higher education as classical education — education in the humanities, education as a civilizing process — have a distinctly nostalgic air. Our Victorian reformer has thankfully also been spared those breathless spectacles appearing on the modern television screen, on which, it has been calculated, the average American youngster will have taken in, some 6,000 scenes of mayhem and murder before reaching the age of fourteen. The amount of 'high culture', even where it is readily available, that the ordinary man willingly imbibes is apparently very limited. In contrast, the amount of unadulterated bilge (judged by any reasonable artistic standards) he can stomach is apparently unlimited. Since the high hopes once entertained by our distinguished forbears have been rudely shattered, the modern humanist or liberal is left with a lot of explaining to do. In the meantime he may dredge some comfort from the thought that if, in existing socialist countries, mass entertainment is not so sick and vulgar as it is in the West, it is still heavily larded with party propaganda.

Notwithstanding the disillusions mentioned above, I believe that there is an irrespressible propensity for the modern mind — the mind of the ordinary citizen and even the mind of the thinking man in the last half of the twentieth century — to overvalue the benefits conferred on the human race by science and technology and to underrate and extenuate their destructive power. This is partly because in a society of relative abundance, the ubiquity of advertizing media acts to direct men's thoughts of what constitutes self-betterment towards worldly things, towards material achievement, status, and towards the things that money can buy. Consequently, they attach disproportionate value to these components of well-being. Indeed, in making invidious comparisons between past and present, neither is the journalistic historian free from this bias. How often are we exhorted to imagine what life would be like without electricity or without all those modern conveniences that make life so comfortable! 'Just picture how dull and confining life would be without modern means of travel and communication!'

The Transience of Novelty
But if we are to exercise our imaginations in making invidious comparisons between past and present, there are some additional facts of life to be borne in mind. The pleasure afforded by novelty — the theme on which so much advertizing turns — is necessarily ephemeral. It would not be too harsh a judgement to say that the morale of the citizen of post-war affluence is coming to depend upon a succession of novelties — upon 'new experiences', 'new sensations', 'new thrills' — as a drug-addict comes to depend for his self-assurance on a succession of shots. And frequent fashion-changes help to maintain the illusion of continuous novelty; not only fashion changes in clothes but also in cars and furniture. In fact every conceivable device or toy is remodelled every year or so by hard-working design departments.

Yet even when the novelty is quite genuine, even when it is regarded as a miracle of technology, it does not live up to the anticipations of pleasure. As Roszack remarks somewhere in his *Where the Wasteland Ends* (1978), a century ago people would have thrilled to the idea of travelling in a flying machine from one country to another. Today air travel is regarded by many as an ordeal, and by most as a continuous struggle against boredom — in which struggle we are fitfully assisted by liquor, magazines, taped music, films and plastic-tasting tid-bits. The delight once generated by the introduction of the 'gramophone', the stereo, the transister, the cassette, the television, has given way to a routine and listless submission. I cannot believe that a future in which we hurtle through space in rockets will provide any more enduring entertainment than travelling by air does today; at all events, the view from the rocket windows — black space punctuated by distant glimmers — is not likely to fascinate us long. Those whose hopes for a joyous life are premised on excitements and novelties yet to come will eventually find themselves fighting tedium in order to escape despair.

The Costs of Ease
Another fact of life is no less telling in this connection. The successful pursuit of a life of physical ease, realized through a succession of labour-saving innovations, which appears to be shunting our civilization towards a push-button utopia, is not merely self-defeating, it is subversive of human well-being. Put aside the ill effects on our health from leading lives far more sedentary than nature ever intended us to do, and bear with the thought that life cannot be fully enjoyed save through contrasts. Central heating, for instance, passes for a convenience that is now available to almost everyone in the West. But gone is the joy of warming to the blaze of a log fire, especially after having been out in the cold cutting up the wood, and while so occupied cheerful in anticipation of the crackle and glow of the fire to come.

As the historian Huizinga writes of the Middle Ages, 'We, at the present-day, can hardly understand the keenness with which a fur coat, a good fire on the hearth, a soft bed, a glass of wine, were formerly enjoyed' For there can be no real gratification without prior effort of frustration. True friendships, comradeship, spring up between men sharing common dangers or facing hardships together: they are not formed on package tours.

Recall that only in Aldous Huxley's *Brave New World* were all sources of hardship and frustration removed. And the outcome was a population of emotional cretins. Since there was no sublimation of the sex drive in the *Brave New World*, there was no romance either. Since there was no danger, neither were there any heroes. There was no occasion for discipline, and no call for sacrifice. And consequently there was no poetry, and no aspiration to the good and the beautiful.

EPILOGUE: THE CURSE OF PROMETHEUS

The Non-Neutrality of Science
I end these reflections with what will doubtless pass muster for a reactionary view of scientific progress. Certainly, I maintain that science, or at any rate the spirit animating scientific enquiry, is inherently incompatible with any traditional conception of religion. I maintain further that this science has underwritten a technology that wrecks any prospect of the good life, and has capped this achievement by placing the survival of man, indeed of the planet itself, in imminent danger.

I brush aside impatiently the standard pretext that science itself is neutral — that it is left to man himself to decide whether to use the discoveries of science for benevolent or malevolent purposes. One reason for my impatience is that the products of scientific research, even when they are believed put to good uses, often result in damage or disaster, and sometimes in irremediable disaster, simply because unsuspected, perhaps unforeseeable, adverse consequences also arise from their use. As mentioned earlier, scientists just do not know the range of consequences of a growing number of new drugs, additives, synthetics, pesticides, and so on. In all innocence we sprayed large parts of the earth with DDT. Later on, and notwithstanding works like Rachel Carson's *Silent Spring,* agribusiness began to use more deadly pesticides. Again, physicians in Europe took to sedating pregnant women with the new wonder drug Thalidomide, as a result of which many thousands of families are now condemned to suffer the prolonged anguish of having to rear deformed children.

Another reason for my scorn of such pretexts is that scientists also, and quite knowingly, seek to produce innovations that are unambiguously destructive. They dedicate their talents to discovering more effective means of bacteriological warfare, more paralyzing gases, more powerful nuclear warheads and neutron bombs, and so on. And even where there is clear choice in the use of a new method or product — as dynamite, for example, useful for blasting rock in building a highway, can also be used for blowing up people, or the laser beam, which can be used in industry to cut through the hardest metals can be used also as a death ray by the military or by criminals and terrorists — one can be sure that, in a world erupting with fanaticism and violence, the uses to which it will be put will often enough be purely destructive.

The Spirit of Science and the Death of Religion
I assert, finally, that the spirit of science is antithetical to, indeed subversive of, the spirit of religion. For we either believe our religion to be true or we believe nothing. And how can we be believe in God today! Once the ethos of science comes to dominate the human mind; once, that is, people come to accept that every phenomenon has a 'natural' cause; that it is the duty and the destiny of science to uncover all nature's secrets; that 'free inquiry' is sacred; and that all statements or beliefs, whatever their character or provenance, must yield to the test of a scientifically approved methodology — why then, all the great myths that for millennia have sustained the human spirit are effectively undermined.

In short, the sacralization of life cannot go hand-in-hand with its secularization. God becomes expendable in a science-based civilization; becomes transmuted into a metaphor — encouraged by churchmen such as Bishop Robinson. There may be exultation among humanists, among technocrats and among the scientists themselves (apparently always on the verge of a new 'break-through'). But for the ordinary mortal who prefers to believe, nay who needs to believe, but is no longer able to, the loss is irreparable. Today, the ordinary man, the man-in-the-automobile, the insatiate creature of a hyper-commercial civilization, garlanded with gadgetry, festooned with technological frou-frou, is now also prone to glimpses of despair. Bereft of a sustaining faith, he struggles to repress the prospect of his journey towards the dread moment of his final and total extinction.

As Kierkegard has written, 'If there were no external consciousness in a man, if at the foundation of all there lay only a wild seething power which, writhing with obscure passions, produced everything that is great and everything that is insignificant; if a bottomless void never satiated lay hidden beneath all — what then would life be but despair?'

Science Seen As Faustian Lust

Despite its triumphs, some of us see science today in a light quite different from that in which it is wont to bask, and to discover in its monstrous proportions a character and a purpose scarcely suspected. Just how much of its self-assessment is hypocrisy and how much self-deception, is difficult to determine.

Ice-cool, dispassionate, all-penetrating, all-controlled and with pious whisperings of the common good, of its ordained mission that must be fulfilled. With overspread hands, beneath the jet of holy waters, intoning its sacred right to uncover all of every stitch of nature, to chart every breathing pulse in the living universe, to capture every fluttering beat that else might escape, to expose every particle and cell to the pitiless glare of its great cormorant eye — an eye like Lucifer's possessed of a raging unquenchable lust for knowledge. And even now, heedless, it quests on 'with compulsion and laborious flight' to its own destruction.

This raging spirit of science has ripped the warm mysterious darkness from the soul of the earth. It has spun its computerized web and has mantled the globe with a myriad flickering lights, electronic bleeps, battalions of grinning symbols, slowly strangling the throb of the human voice. It freezes resistance on the instant with the promise of glinting power. For this satanic science is determined to leave nothing unslit; not a sliver of flesh, nothing. Its jaws are set to crunch and to burst open every close secret of nature, every once-wondrous mystery; to scotch every flight of fancy, every source of myth and magical belief that for so long inspired hope and rejoicing in the heart of our forbears. All has now to be prised open, the temple treasures ransacked, the juice of life spilt, the earth's fragrance dispersed and the last veils of mystery and wonder cut through, chewed to tatters, until naught remains to discover and destroy — naught but to weep alone in the cold of annihilation's waste.

It is not, then, the noble Prometheus, the darling of science, that is the hero of the human adventure on earth. That legend is man's flattering unction of himself, his cosetted self-image, a legend he clings to so that he may, when the day of reckoning comes, whisper cringingly that 'Oh, he did it all for the best, to ease the lot and to relieve the suffering of his fellow men'. In all the tortuous record of human self-deception there can hardly be a more superb instance — Faustian lust masquerading as dedication to the altar of truth.

Science, Technology and Malaise

To conclude, there is no doubt that something like alarm and dismay has begun to creep over our Western civilization. The mood of the public fluctuates, but the whiff of foreboding persists. Something serious seems to be going awry, something that transcends our current economic difficulties.

I suggest that we should be wrong to seek explanations for this malaise in capitalism *per se,* much less in the operation of the market. Explanations are to be sought, instead, in the unfolding consequences of science and technology over the last century and more especially since the end of the Second World War.

There is no need today to remind people that humanity lives precariously, close to the brink of a nuclear Armageddon. For we have, finally, learned to think of the unthinkable. The so-called balance of terror hardly looks like a stable equilibrium at this point of time. One false step, one too hasty reaction to a reckless threat, could start the conflagration. And in a world where smaller countries currently ruled by tyrants and fanatics, will soon come to possess the means of atomic destruction, that one false step looks frighteningly close.

But even if our civilization should survive such imminent physical perils, the prospects for humanity are far from promising. Mounting public anxiety in all the countries of the Western bloc about the dangers of new technologies and their products, and about the associated upsurge of crime, is sure to augment the size and power of governments, and so reduce our personal freedoms.

For the rest, we pay dear for our technological toys. The centrifugal forces of technical progress have sundered the filaments of the once-intricate web of custom. The pervasive sense of kinship and loyalty, of pride and propriety, the unquestioned acceptance of duties and privilege, of those mutual obligations that marked the more traditional and hierarchical society, have all but vanished. In its place we find the virtues attributable to modern economic man — the motivated man, the insatiate man, the uprooted man, the hedonistic man, the godless man, the man who acts on the principle of net advantages. What human warmth remains is generated in the main through inter-group hostilities, through perpetual political jostling, through the claims and recriminations of new ethnic minorities and self-styled liberation movements.

Thus personal relations once rooted in mutual trust are everywhere giving way today to formal contracts that render mutual trust obsolete. Even within families, just and proper treatment can no longer rely on accepted obligations or be referred to immemorial custom. Recourse is had to litigation and enforcement agencies.

As morality shrinks, legislation expands, and as the peripheral support system of formalities, courtesies and conventions — uncongenial to the pace and turnover of modern life — atrophies, whatever is needed to prevent minor frictions and conflicts is done by state regulation and central direction. Indeed, in modern Western communities, the emerging population of self-seeking atomistic units, highly mobile, highly motivated, increasingly conscience-free, can be held together as a people, as a nation, only through an expanding bureaucracy, its rulings enforced through the ultimate agency of an increasingly powerful police.

Knowledge and The Fall of Man

A final reflection. The human adventure just might have turned out otherwise. If one speculates, as does Lynn White, on the connection between the Judaeo-Christian religious tradition (which confers on man, as God's supreme creature, dominion over all forms of life) and the subsequent exploratory and exploitive nature of his activity (which has extended his power over nature to an awesome degree), another route is imaginable, one that does not lead to the present impasse.

Pagan and tribal religions did not, for the most part, envisage man as the paragon of the universe, but as no more than a component part of nature, one creature among an uncountable number of different creatures, one form of life among a limitless variety. As such, the savage had a reverence not only for all life but also for all things in nature. A tree, a spring, a rock, was not to him an inanimate object. It had spirit of its own, a place in the universe. What a man needed from the earth for his own survival had to be taken with care, with respect, sometimes with conciliatory prayer or ceremony.[5] One had to placate the spirit within all things to ensure that one's own spirit should not be violated.

Had such an attitude towards life prevailed throughout the world, civilizations or organized communities would not have advanced very far by the lights of modern achievement. We should be inclined to refer to such communities as 'static' or, worse, as 'stagnant'. But it would be parochial to dismiss the idea that a necessary condition for global survival is that the civilizations that emerge remain static — after advancing to some level of technology, that is, and then remaining in a steady state. A dynamic civilization — dynamic in the technological sense, that is — looks to be inherently unstable. It is impelled ever onwards to a stage where eventually it cannot draw back from the precipice — even, as now, when the precipice comes into view.

We are told in the Scriptures that 'the love of money is the root of all evil'. And this is surely so in the diurnal drama of human affairs. But, in today's global context, and thinking poignantly of the small planet earth that is man's heritage, and his only refuge in a dark, cold and inhospitable universe, it is surely the love of *knowledge*, of scientific knowledge, that is the root of all evil — and the seed of his self-destruction.

NOTES

1. The Reverend Sidney Smith, one of the founders and editors of the *Edinburgh Review,* whose satirical pen advanced the cause of reform in Britain, was also something of a *bon vivant* and one of the most celebrated wits of his day. A frequent visitor of the sumptuous gatherings of the great Whig houses, he was a particular friend of Lord and Lady Holland.

    Although Sidney was ordained deacon in 1794, he felt at the time no calling for the Church. Indeed, he wished to follow his elder brother in a career at the bar, but his father refused to finance his legal training.

2. *See* the article 'Obscenity and Maturity', *The Sunday Times* (14 December 1969) by Dr John Robinson (formerly Bishop of Woolwich), which by any standards is a model of vacuity, ambiguity and inconclusiveness.

3. Reasons for this conclusion are given in my essay 'The Road to Repression', (Ch. 6 in this volume).

4. The damage wont to be associated with the exposure of workers to a contaminating atmosphere is held to be undervalued as evidence accumulates to show that exposure can result not only from inhalation but also from absorption through the skin and the digestive organs.

5. In Carlos Castaneda's *Road to Xtlian*, Don Juan lays a net to trap birds for a meal and succeeds in catching six of them. To the consternation of the author, however, he lets four birds free since the two remaining would suffice to remove their hunger: one does not take the life of a creature simply to gorge oneself.

Index